Conversation Tactics

Techniques to Confront, Challenge, and Resolve With Grace (Book 2)

Difficult Conversations Made Painless

By Patrick King, Social Interaction Specialist
at www.PatrickKingConsulting.com

Table of Contents

Introduction

Someone had parked in my spot again. *Seriously?*

At one of my first jobs we had the privilege of assigned parking spots. This definitely wasn't an indication of a high-status job – it just indicated the management's successful method in making us accept a lower wage by giving us new hires parking spots.

But hey, I was a teenager and the notion sounded sufficiently brag-worthy, so the tradeoff seemed worthwhile for me.

The only problem was that a month after I started, a red Honda Civic kept parking in my spot and forcing me to search for parking every morning. It was a small parking lot so it's not like I had to walk much farther, but it was the principle of the thing. The driver of the red Honda was intentionally and maliciously parking in my spot, despite the fact that he or she knew it was assigned to someone else.

What kind of person would do that? It was unfathomable to me that someone would be that self-centered.

I started to come in before my shift just to try to catch the culprit, but it seemed like since that month started, the car was always there before me. For weeks I fumed to my friends about how angry I was at the driver of the red Honda and just how I would tell them off when I finally caught them.

In my mind, the maliciousness and overall ugliness of the offender grew with each day. He or she probably had chronic dandruff and a case of incurable unibrow.

Being fully committed to my goal of exposing this person, I arrived to work 90 minutes early one cold, Monday morning and was finally able to park in the empty spot. I saw the offender, and let's just say he wasn't quite who I expected.

It was the company janitor. He was over 60 years old and barely spoke English. It was clear that even if he had been told by management that the parking spots were assigned, he didn't understand and covered it up by smiling and nodding.

He parked in the spot next to me and I got out of my car and greeted him good morning. Of course, he responded to this by smiling and nodding.

I began to seriously rethink all of my misdirected anger for the past few weeks.

This is a book about difficult conversations and how to handle confrontation with grace and minimize tension. There are so many steps to approaching a difficult conversation that begin before the fact, and this situation with the parking spot clearly demonstrates a couple of very important ones.

First, I would have saved a lot of unnecessary emotion and anger were I able to separate intent from impact. In other words, I thought just because someone did something, they meant to offend or disregard me. This is a toxic way of thinking and completely ignores the fact most of us aren't intentionally evil on a daily basis.

Second, whether you think you are totally in the right, you aren't. There is your story, the other party's story, and the third story – the third story is the real sequence of events. Before and during a difficult conversation, this should be the primary focus instead of lashing out at the other person.

Many people see confrontation and conflict as huge and rare events, but the truth is that most of our conflict stems from everyday situations. Knowing how to address those situations with Conversation Tactics can eliminate interpersonal anxiety and tension from your life.

Luckily for both me and the janitor, I was able to catch myself before directing my anger into something harmful and embarrassing.

People will go to shockingly great lengths to avoid a difficult conversation. Aren't there some weights you'd like off your chest?

Chapter 1. The Why of Difficult Conversations

No matter how charming you are, not every conversation you partake in is going to be a pleasure.

Now, this means one of two things. First, it means that you might not enjoy the people you are talking to. This happens frequently.

Second, and more importantly, it means that some of your conversations are by nature difficult, awkward, and confrontational. When you need to talk to your co-worker about how she talks too much, or to your significant other about how you need more space when you are with your friends – these are not easy conversations for anyone.

You know what you want to say, and you know the message you want to convey, but there are so many possible missteps when emotions and confrontation are involved. People get hurt, become defensive, and feel judged. Thus passive aggressive behavior and avoidance is fanned into a relationship.

This was a daily struggle when I was a practicing lawyer. It's a profession built upon condescending insults masked behind civil remarks, which presents its own unique challenge.

A major part of being a good conversationalist is the ability to handle difficult conversations when they arise and when they *need* to arise. Whether you like to admit it or not, dealing with verbal tension is an important skill that can lead to your ascension to that corner office and the most rewarding relationship of your life – or a dead-end job and a string of frigid, failed relationships.

That's the unpredictable beauty of the human condition.

Guess who is great at handling sticky and uncomfortable situations? Leaders. These are people we admire and respect for their courage and strength. And it's time for you to join their ranks.

Others might not always like you, but that doesn't matter. You're doing something they don't think they can do, something which may be inherently difficult. That's how respect and admiration is earned: perseverance and taking on difficult situations others stray away from.

You may not think someone is a better person for running marathons, but you cannot deny the effort and dedication they need to run them. That's the kind of feeling you'll impart when you are able to handle confrontation and difficult conversations without a problem.

Difficult Conversations Make You a Better Communicator

A big advantage of consciously preparing difficult conversations is that you will learn how to express exactly what you want and make people feel heard. These are the building blocks of great communicators.

Confrontation is best handled carefully. You need to account for large emotional spikes. Learning to deal with those artfully, and in a way that acknowledges, but diffuses, emotion is how you can reach the true heart of any matter. You'll be able to step around egos and pride, which are huge detriments to honest communication.

Have you ever fought with your significant other? If you were able to just cut through the clutter and figure out that he or she was simply upset about how often you washed the dishes, you would be able to save a lot of time and effort.

Mastering difficult conversations enables you to be a better conversationalist as well. You will learn how to read people and know exactly what you can say, and what you shouldn't say at certain times. You'll be able to create a feeling of safety and vulnerability which is helpful in all walks of life.

Diffuse Tension Before it Grows

Another great reason for mastering difficult conversations is that when you bottle up tensions, they can reach dangerous levels very quickly. You can only suppress it for so long. This is why people seem to suddenly blow up over the most trivial of things.

Everyone has a finite amount of tension they can suppress

before it has to be expressed in one way or another. For some, they can let some out through activities like boxing or painting. However, it doesn't mean that they have an excuse to not address difficult topics.

The worst conversations occur because one of the participants has done their damndest to avoid it. They prolong the process and hope that either they can successfully bury their emotions or the situation will diffuse itself without them.

Once they actually express themselves, they feel like an enormous weight has been lifted from their shoulders. Every party involved always feels better after the difficult conversation, though perhaps not during.

In the end, life is short, so it's a waste to feel like you're carrying a burden every day. A conversation about washing the dishes might be just that on day one, but by day fifteen, it's going to be a host of other resentments.

Avoid Passive Aggressive Behavior

Passive aggressive behavior is a toxic behavior that occurs when you try to suppress your dissatisfaction with something. It's essentially impossible to suppress with 100% effectiveness, so passive aggression is what escapes your filters and lets other people know that you are upset.

The longer you put something off, the more tension builds inside, and the more passive aggressive behavior occurs. If you address a difficult conversation sooner rather than later you can avoid these little daggers that have the ability to end friendships and relationships.

Sometimes you can't even help it. It's a personal jab here, a snarky comment there, or a questionably deliberate act over yonder. It leaks out like a balloon that is inflated more and more each day. The habit of passive aggression seeps into our mindsets easily and sometimes seizes the entire tone of the relationship.

By simply deciding to deal with difficult conversations directly, this can open the floodgates to you totally vaporizing passive aggressive strategies as an option in all areas of your life.

Confrontation Is Positive

Not all confrontations begin and end like fighters in a boxing ring. And they shouldn't.

Confrontation is healthy and positive. It challenges us and makes us act our best at all times, even when we might not want to.

Confrontation is *not* to be avoided at all costs.

Don't seek it out, but don't stray from it because it can be your greatest teacher. If you don't deal with something as it happens, you will just deal with the enlarged, reinforced version later. Sadly, by the time you get around to dealing with it, it is twice the size and its negative impact is thrice the size. You're just making things harder for yourself by waiting and hoping that things will blow over. They won't.

Stand your ground and don't be afraid to be the first to speak up. Confrontation is how the people in your life know you respect them and you are worthy of their respect. Otherwise, they lack any meaningful feedback and your relationships will suffer accordingly from a special type of dishonesty.

Difficult conversations make people look at themselves in the mirror. You're letting them see a perspective of reality that they may be totally blind to. These people probably need to see that other angle and other story. And so do you for yourself.

It may be unwelcome and it may be the last thing that they want to hear, but always remember that you are doing them a favor by showing them your perspective. This may be the wakeup call that they need. It's usually unwelcome, but it's absolutely necessary. Don't be afraid to be the person that gives them that message, or hears the message for yourself.

Practice Candidness

Being candid and calling life the way you see it are good habits.

Often, you'll be saying things that other people are thinking and you'll find that you have a lot more in common than you think you might.

The simple act of saying what you want and think in a candid, yet respectful, manner makes what you want in life possible. There is rarely any receiving without asking.

You'll also see whom among the people around you are truly your friends. If you can't be candid among your friends, then when are you ever expressing your true thoughts?

The people that can't stand your inner thoughts are entitled to their opinions. So you'll repel them, but attract the people that love the true, candid you.

Tackle the Inevitable

If you try to suppress bad news or uncomfortable truths, you're not doing anybody any favors. By sweeping things under the rug, the reality will still be there. The worst part is, it will build up to such a degree over time that when it finally blows up, you make it all that much more painful for you and the people that you thought you were protecting.

Do them a favor by airing out uncomfortable truths now while they are still small.

I wrote this to teach you how to have difficult conversations in such a way that you help build other people up, while at the same time ensuring relationships stay intact. It may seem like an impossible tightrope to walk, but it's really a question of technique and finesse. All it takes is a phrase here or there to really make the difference in the message you are conveying.

Difficult conversations ensure that relationships are built on a solid bedrock of honesty. How would you feel if your friend revealed to you that she has hated eating with you for the past five years because of your manners? It's likely something you'd rather have heard about and rectified five years ago. The past five years might feel like a lie.

If you have a full and open conversation among equal adults in a relationship, that relationship will flourish because it's based on mutual trust and respect. Honesty is the fuel of a real mature and solid relationship. There are no two ways about it. The truth can set you free, though it can definitely sting at first. If you both are mature enough to establish a relationship on the right footing, things will look great for both your relationship and your development as mature adults.

The lengths people will go so they can avoid confrontation are vast. Don't let your life be influenced by others to that degree.

Chapter 2. Grant Emotional and Logical Validation

The first step to any difficult conversation is to grant the other person a level of emotional and logical validation, no matter the circumstances. It's a prerequisite to dialogue.

Validation must be present in your conversation or it will stall immediately. What does this mean?

Validation is when you acknowledge what the other person is saying and let them know that you don't think they are stupid or inconsiderate. Chances are, they aren't.

What caused the conflict was the fact an interpretation of events made sense to them logically and emotionally from their point of view. It is valid and you just happen to differ on that interpretation.

Just because you think that something is valid doesn't necessarily mean that you fully agree with it, or that you agree with it at all. It simply means you acknowledge that person's side and you see where they're coming from.

This is something you must convey at the beginning. If you

don't, you run the risk of lunging at someone in an accusatory manner, such as "You're wrong, you're at fault" to which most people will blindly defend themselves. This is a mode where people aren't open to listening to you. To them, there is really no point in them sharing their perspective because they believe you're going to dismiss it outright.

Emotional and logical validation walk hand in hand. If you're able to validate a person on both these counts at the outset, you are positioning yourself for a productive and respectful conversation. Respect is the foundation of any solid discourse.

Logical Validation

Logical validation is when you make people feel that you understand how they arrived at their conclusion.

You paint them as a reasonable person and make them feel understood. You trace the different premises or facts that they used and tie it in with their logical process, and also acknowledge how your actions contributed to that. You understand how they got from A to B to Z.

You are generally saying, "Yes, I can definitely see how someone would think that, and I know I was wrong for my part in it."

If you want to have a difficult conversation about the division of labor around the house, you might say something like "Yes, it makes sense because I was lazy and traveling, you would conclude that I was giving up on my cleaning duties. If I was in your shoes, I would draw that conclusion as well."

There are a couple of important parts here.

First, you give someone a reason to lower their guard when you simply admit that you contributed to the problem. No problem is 100% caused by one party, so it's likely that you might be wrong to some degree. You establish that what you did had an impact on them and they came up with a certain conclusion that you yourself might have found.

Second, you clearly acknowledge that you aren't judging them or tuning them out. You're sheltering them under your opinion that you would do the same in their position. That's powerful for someone to hear.

Flat out state that their viewpoint can have a point and can be both logical and reasonable, given the circumstances of how they look at the situation.

People will usually be extremely worked up because they've had to either pump themselves up to talk about these matters, or they feel attacked. When you acknowledge that they are logically reasonable, you'll see a visible calm and relaxation wash over their body.

That's because they now know that they're not in for an argument or debate, rather a calm discussion where they don't feel attacked. Guess what happens when you don't logically validate right off the bat?

Emotional Validation

The other side of the equation is the realm of feelings.

You can't just address how someone came up with their conclusion based on your actions. You also have to address their emotional reaction. That's the part that you need to tread most carefully with.

Human beings are composed of both logical and emotional processes. For people to feel that you understand them, you have to address both these points.

Emotional validation is acknowledging and respecting that the other person's feelings are valid. Where logical validation says "I understand why you came to that conclusion," emotional validation says "I sympathize with your emotions because I would feel the same if I was you."

Let them know in no uncertain terms that they aren't crazy or unreasonable to feel the way they do.

This is important because conversations are made difficult due to the inherent emotions involved. They are generally negative, and they mostly confuse intent with impact. In other words, most reactions don't account for the fact that every party is trying to act reasonably and without malice.

But that's hard to focus on when people are upset. By validating someone emotionally and you can reduce a situation to a misunderstanding as opposed to an attack. As mentioned with logical validation, this serves to disarm people and immediately make it easier for them to listen to you.

No one likes being painted as crazy or emotionally unstable. We usually don't have that perception of ourselves, so you have to prevent conveying that message by emotionally validating them.

You can also use phrases such as "That sucks. I'd be so angry if I was you," and "I totally get it. What I did was insulting."

Just by making people feel understood on a consistent basis, you might be able to avoid additional consequences. Take into consideration people's history and how circumstances might affect them differently.

Validate Properly

What's the overall purpose of validating someone at the beginning (or before) of a difficult conversation?

It puts them in a place where they can listen to you. It creates the possibility for a dialogue as opposed to a screaming match or argument. When negative emotions are heightened, it might only take one word to rub someone the wrong way and completely derail a conversation.

Validation also inherently shifts some of the blame onto yourself, which is important for people to hear. It shows a degree of responsibility and accountability that makes people feel like the problem at hand can and will be worked out. They'll feel understood.

Listen without interrupting the other person and try to put

labels on their feelings, regardless if they have or haven't done the same for you. It's okay to be harsh with yourself, for example, saying "You mean when I was acting like an asshole it made you feel ignored?" when they might not want to be so blunt. Identify what the other person is feeling, step into their shoes, and feel their perspective.

A good example of this is to say, "I'm sensing that this brought up real feelings of betrayal." This may seem difficult to swallow, but remember that just because you don't agree with their feelings doesn't mean you cannot relate or understand them. You're simply restating what they're expressing from their perspective. Making sure that you know what they're feeling is the key to opening up a difficult conversation.

Establish a solid foundation of emotional and logical validation early in the conversation. If you can't, chances are that you are lying to yourself and stubbornly not admitting any fault. The other person might feel like they are wasting time by speaking with you, and they might be right.

You may think that by doing this you are letting go of your principles or losing right off the bat. That's exactly the type of mindset that leads to explosive conflicts and burnt bridges.

You're not pandering or telling them what they want to hear, you're setting the stage for what you want to say.

Chapter 3. Find the Third Story

I'm reminded of a time when I was walking down a sidewalk in San Francisco.

I was catching up with a friend over the phone and didn't realize I was walking slower than a sleepy snail. This must have been very frustrating for the people behind me, and it wasn't until one of them rudely pushed past me and cursed me that I was broken out of my trance.

I angrily told my friend on the phone that some rude person just couldn't wait two seconds to get by me and didn't have to push me to the side.

It wasn't until later that night that I realized that even though I couldn't see the line forming behind me, I was at fault for impeding strangers on the sidewalk.

How does this relate to difficult conversations? Sometimes we think we are completely in the right and are just victims of a misunderstanding. That's your story.

Their story is that it's your fault, that I was a bumbling

buffoon intentionally walking slowly.

And just like me on the sidewalk, the root of any difficult conversation is a third story – a version where both parties are wrong and right to varying degrees ranging from 1% to 99%.

<u>Find the Third Story</u>

When you are having a difficult conversation with someone, the first thing that you should look for after you've established logical and emotional validation is to search for that third story.

The inherent assumption here is that both parties are wrong and have miscommunicated, and you are simply searching for where that disconnect occurred.

The third story is the explanation that accounts for why one party is hurt or displeased and all the factors that each party contributed to it.

For example, the third story from my experience on the sidewalk is that I didn't realize I was walking slowly, and someone was having a bad day so they felt the need to push me to the side to reach their destination more quickly.

As you can see, the third story is told through the perspective of an innocent third party that has no investment in the outcome. This person is completely impartial.

Pretend there is a third person in the room and imagine

what they would say. What would a judge or mediator come up with based on the evidence presented by both sides?

The third story integrates elements of both stories, but casts no blame on either party. It simply creates reasons to account for the reactions that each party has had. In this way, you are never 100% correct and you are always 1% at fault.

If you are able to accept this, then the third story is possible. If you're going to dismiss any possibility of you being wrong, then the third story is not going to happen, and neither will any productive discourse.

If you're serious about becoming a master of difficult conversations, you need to get used to the chance that in any confrontation you may be 1% wrong.

Accept the Third Story

The secret to finding the third story and accepting it is adopting the right mindset. Be of the mindset that you're inquiring. Think of yourself as a sort of reporter and you're trying to get to the bottom of a story. If you're able to assume that mindset, then the third story is not just possible, but probable.

You have to look at what the other person is saying, along with what you're feeling and thinking, and try to piece everything together the way a journalist would. Ask yourself exactly how and what made you and the other person feel this way. What logical and emotional conclusion must have been reached that both of you were not aware of?

By putting all the facts that were discussed by both parties through a logical blender, you can come up with bits and pieces that can be reassembled like a jigsaw puzzle to fit a third story.

The beauty about the third story is that it sidesteps the very thorny issue of assigning blame. People don't like to be wrong. Everyone wants to be right.

Now, the conversation is no longer about conflict. Instead, the conversation is figuring out what assumptions, leaps, and logic were involved on both sides that created the situation. This way, your focus is more on process instead of conclusion.

Acknowledging how others see the issue, focusing on the process, and letting them also see how they came to certain conclusions, you can piece together a third story. Borrowing enough from all of your personal processes, you can form the third story each person in the conversation can be happy with.

Benefit of the Doubt

I know that for some people this is very hard to accept, but you have to swallow your pride and assume that there's nothing fundamentally wrong with the other person/party cognitively, mentally, or emotionally.

The next hard pill to swallow is that you in some way caused the issue,. Always assume this. The other party is likely just as reasonable as you and that there is something that created their version of the story.

Without this mindset, the third story is not going to materialize. Your own conception of who and what the other person is gets in the way of piecing together details to put a third story together.

The third story is really all about comparison.

When you lay side by side both parties' versions of what happened and their conclusions, you can then see where the disconnect lies and where there is overlap. The point of overlap is the launching pad to a logical and emotionally sufficient third story that both parties can somehow or someway accept.

Here are some helpful phrases to use in evoking the third story:
- Can we just start from the beginning and figure out what happened?
- What caused us to react like that in that situation?
- So what exactly did I do to make you feel that way?
- What happened in-between X and Y?
- What would someone who was just observing us say about what happened?

Chapter 4. Separate Impact from Intent

Last year, one of my female friends went through a period of weight gain due to a legitimate thyroid problem.

She met up with an old college friend that she hadn't seen in years, and the college friend said the worst thing she possibly could have: *"You're pregnant! When's the baby due?"*

This obviously did not go over well, but it illustrates the difference between impact and intent.

When you are faced with a negative situation, the situation itself is the impact. The intent is whether you believe someone meant to inflict the damage or not, and unfortunately, much of the time we assume that the intent matches the impact.

Intent is what a person means to do. Intent is what the person is thinking when they are in the process of saying or doing something. Their thoughts speak to what they wish to happen and the consequences they wish to cause. Impact is the consequences of an action or speech regardless of the actor's intent.

In other words, my friend probably assumed that the negative impact of being called fat was intended by her friend, but that was nowhere close to the truth.

When someone does or says something nasty to you, it can be difficult to move beyond the pain and clearly separate intent from crushing impact. In a majority of cases, people aren't being malicious or hurtful – they are oblivious at best.

Try to focus on the separation between these two factors so that you can get some emotional distance from the topic of your discussion. Being able to mentally and emotionally separate impact from intent can go a long way in your efforts at having difficult conversations with people.

In the vast majority of cases, the perpetrator's intent doesn't always line up with the impact on the victim. That's where the saying "the path to hell is paved with good intentions" comes from. People with good intentions create negative circumstances every day. That doesn't make them bad people.

For example, a landlord decides not to the renew the lease of a tenant whose children always leave the yard a mess. Instead of negotiating with the tenant, the landlord insists on the tenant leaving so he or she can find someone without children who will take care of the yard.

The landlord's intent is to keep the property clean, but the impact is that a family with young children must uproot and find a new place to live, which might be far more difficult than the landlord assumes.

Or more simply, your roommate decides to cook Indian food for you because they thought they heard you say you loved it, but in actuality you were saying that you were highly, highly allergic to it. His or her intent did not match the impact.

People Operate on Impact

As well-intentioned as you might be, the sad reality is that the world only cares about what you actually do. Your impact.

Do your grades depend on the fact that you knew the answer but wrote down the wrong one? Does your job performance depend on the fact that you wanted to stay late to fix some things, but decided to go to a movie instead? No and no. You don't get extra credit for thinking the right thing but doing something wrong.

The world only cares about the results that you deliver. It's unlikely that someone can figure out exactly what you're thinking at a particular point in time. No one can read your mind, and all too often we assume that the hints we drop are glaringly obvious. If that were the case, wouldn't we all be a little bit better at dealing with the opposite sex?

When you are thinking of having a difficult conversation with somebody, focus on this separation between impact and intent. Focus on what they actually said, and only that, not how you felt about it.

Don't try to read intent into what was going inside their head. in many cases, you don't fully know these people. In many cases, you don't know them at all, and suddenly you are playing mind-reader.

Think about how annoyed you are when people judge your actions, assuming you meant something one way when you meant the complete opposite.

When you're having a difficult conversation about something you did, don't automatically assume that people can get inside your head and figure out what your motivations were, and whether or not your intentions were in the right place.

None of that matters. They can only see what they see. This is where the judgment comes from. They can only judge you based on the actions they saw.

Assume Good Intentions

Despite the fact people only operate on impact, that's a tough way to approach a difficult conversation.

Start difficult conversations with an assumption of positive, or at least neutral, intentions in the face of negative impact. At worst, assume ignorance and carelessness than intentional evil or malice. The former hurts far less.

This will diffuse the negative thoughts spiraling in your mind and help you focus on the facts of the situation so you can come up with a more objective verdict.

It's easy to jump to the conclusion that the person who did you wrong is a no-good, worthless, and malicious person. But it's going to set back your ability to establish a difficult conversation on a solid foundation of mutual respect and emotional validation.

To put your emotional state at the right place when you're trying to get a difficult conversation going, assume at best ignorance and carelessness instead of malice.

Some phrases to bring the conversation to a place of clarifying intentions and minimizing impact:

- I know you didn't mean it that way, did you?
- What was the purpose or intent behind that?
- I was unaware that you would interpret it that way.
- When you did X, did you mean Y?
- Were you aware that I might see it as X?

Let's say that one of your best friends mistakenly insulted your mother.

Can we give your friend the benefit of the doubt that she is a reasonable person and does not wish to actually insult your mother? Check and check. Start from the point where malice is not in the equation and only miscommunication is.

Chapter 5. Address Causation

When was the last time you were sick?

When you eventually made your way to the doctor, how would you feel in each of the following scenarios?

Scenario A: The doctor sees that you are in pain and just gives you some band-aids and painkillers to deal with it. All he cares about is making you feel better at that moment, so he tells you if the painkillers don't work he will prescribe even stronger ones. There is no mention about preventative care and addressing the symptoms. Eventually, you have emergency surgery to remove your appendix because it wasn't evaluated.

Scenario B: The doctor sees that you are in pain, but works to determine the cause of the pain so that it won't recur. He wants to make sure that you never face this issue again and takes precautions towards the cause and thinks long-term. He runs a thorough battery of tests and diagnoses that you have some appendix issues. He is able to act with preventative care and prevent any further pain.

It might be a combination of A and B, but if he didn't at least mention Scenario B, he was not a very good doctor. It highlights the futility of dealing solely in terms of symptoms instead of root causes. Regardless of the band-aid you use, the root cause will still remain, and the band-aid is liable to fall off at any moment. Where will you be then?

This is the same approach that you must take with difficult conversations. Instead of focusing on the symptoms of an issue, you must focus on the root cause to prevent it from recurring time and time again.

If you only focus on soothing someone's emotional pain, you're not fixing the actual problem. Even if you deal with people's superficial annoyances with you and try to smooth their ruffled feathers, you're not going to make the problem go away. In the future it will be about something else equally petty and you will both have to go through the same ritual again. How many times do you want to go through that process?

For example, buying your significant other an extravagant present to make up for a forgotten anniversary or birthday is dealing with a symptom. Dealing with the root cause is making sure that you have systems or alarms in place to remind you of important dates to become a better partner.

Fighting about who does the dishes or who should get more credit on a work assignment is dealing with the symptoms. Dealing with the root cause is creating a rotation for the chores and a chart for whom gets credit on specific assignments.

By taking out the root cause of the issue, regardless of how inconvenient and potentially risky it would be, you ensure a more conflict-free future.

Think Beyond the Temporary

When you're confronted with an unpleasant emotional reaction, someone crying, for example, it's tempting to create quick relief by appeasing them. Give them their way, buy them something to forget, or try to placate them with a host of concessions.

However, in no way is that helpful for anything beyond that immediate moment. In fact, you are probably creating a problem of epic proportions for later with your continued avoidance.

For example, if your child is always crying, you can deal with the situation (the symptoms) by giving her a piece of candy. By only attempting to make the child stop crying, you don't find out about the cause that your child is actually upset at being bullied at school.

Continued avoidance will lead to a slippery slope of self-esteem and self-worth issues as an adult. You're not doing anyone, your child in particular, any favors by focusing on short-term solutions.

You're actually enabling them and allowing them to cry wolf. You're teaching them how to manipulate you and get the outcome they want without improving the situation.

It's not going to be easy. It's going to require inquisition, introspection, assessment, and tough truths. You have to be mentally and emotionally ready for it.

Find Root Causes

The first step in finding a root cause as opposed to a mere symptom is to ask yourself the following question: "If I address this issue right now, are the chances of the problem recurring affected at all?"

Generally speaking, binge-eating is typically a symptom of low self-esteem and emotional instability, as opposed to willpower and making healthy eating choices. People who binge-eat aren't overweight because they fail to make healthy choices. They are overweight because they can't control their negative emotions and how to cope with them effectively without food. You can't address it simply by removing all the chocolate from their household pantry.

Not doing the dishes might be a symptom of being overworked and long hours. Simply getting a maid won't really help the root cause of that.

It's important to find behavioral patterns, because if symptoms keep arising, it means there is a root cause and it isn't just a coincidence.

Think and be honestly introspective about the "why" of a symptom in your life. Keep going down your list and try to get more explanations by asking, "Where, what, when, how, and why?" and tracing things to the root cause. You might think that one of the items in your list is the root cause, but if you filter all the things on your list through these five basic questions, you'd be surprised as to what you'd find.

You might have a friend that is upset with your lack of recent attention. You might want to solve the problem by devoting one full day to them. This will help, but it doesn't address the root cause of why he or she feels neglected.

Perhaps they feel neglected when they don't get hugs from you, or when they don't hear from you for over a week. Either, or both, could be the root cause.

It is important that you don't engage in this problem looking to assign blame. You're not going to solve the problem that way. Instead, be ready to assess your own contribution to the root cause. What did you do to bring the root cause?

View finding root causes like a giant, impartial puzzle. Assume some emotional distance so you can have enough intellectual firepower to break everything up into small pieces and reassemble them to fit the patterns that keep recurring.

Without emotional distance, you won't make much progress. Without emotional distance, it's too easy for your efforts at finding root issues a personal or accusatory exercise. You're looking for answers. You're not looking people or situations to blame.

Instead of looking for the culprit or perpetrator that did you harm and was malicious, focus instead on how a chain of events brought about consequences that you now have to deal with.

Chapter 6. Tact(ics): Speak So People Will Listen

The difficult part about confrontational conversations is people just don't know what to say.

People like to imagine that there are phrases which will effectively convey their point, yet are also amazingly subtle so as to not cause a reaction. Phrases that will simultaneously be harsh yet create gentle understanding.

People essentially want phrases to confront without the feeling of confrontation.

Unfortunately, that's impossible. You're asking for a Jedi mind trick that doesn't exist and you'll only waste time searching for it. It's like breaking up with someone. We delay because we want to find the right moment and right words, but the words don't really matter when you're delivering that kind of news.

That said, you must possess tact in a difficult conversation and not come down on people like a sledgehammer.

Tact is about positioning what you are about to say to

convey your message, yet dulling the emotional impact. It takes finding the right context and setting the appropriate mood. Of course, it's always a good idea to speak tactfully, but it is absolutely necessary when you're having a difficult conversation.

Tact is the ability to communicate negative issues without the tension. Tact is the ability to tell someone to go to hell and have them excited for the trip. This is important in a difficult conversation because tensions will be high and can easily boil over.

How do you find the thin line between being tactful and completely sugarcoating issues? Tact isn't being dishonest or hiding. Tact is a matter of framing, perspective, and delivery, while sugarcoating often involves deceiving people in an opaque manner.

It requires you to map out the many directions that your speech can take and how it might impact the listener. Most people simply get straight to the point. They don't really care about the impact. They only care about unloading stuff off their chest. From their perspective, this is the quickest way to get from point A to point B.

From the listener's perspective, what they said can be quite offensive, irritating and can produce explosive situations. The simplest and the most direct way to say something may not be the best way if you want to speak tactfully. There is something to be said for such so-called "verbal diarrhea," but it is often a result of suppressed emotion.

There Is No Perfect Line or Time

No ifs, ands, or buts about it.

You have to learn how to speak tactfully if you are going to master the art of the difficult conversation. There's no getting around it, and there is no magic formula to make every situation flow smoothly.

When you avoid a situation by searching and struggling for this magic line, you are only procrastinating and making the situation grow day by day. There will never be a perfect time and set of circumstances to drop a bomb as serious as "I can't stand your mother," or "I am getting really frustrated with our marriage."

There will never be a perfect time to deliver uncomfortable news or rough truths. You can't help this, it's a universal truth of difficult conversations. No matter the setting, time, and words, you will impact someone's mood.

You will have to become comfortable the tension and discomfort associated with confrontation. We've discussed why some confrontation is healthy and can be good for your health. It's up to you whether or not to jump into the pool and start swimming.

There may be no such thing as good settings and times, but there are definitely bad settings and times.

For example, it's not a good idea to have a difficult conversation with somebody involving very uncomfortable truths in public, or in front of other people. It's a bad idea to have a hard conversation with them when they are already having a tough time, when they are already feeling terrible about something else. Don't engage right before you go out somewhere public, or where they might need to concentrate or focus, such as with a big presentation at work or school.

So even though you'll inevitably impact someone's mood and state of mind initially, how you shape the difficult conversation afterwards it us to you.

Avoid Using "You"

When you're delivering a harsh reality to a listener, try to avoid using the word "you."

As much as possible, focus on the word "I." By doing so, you focus on the impact of an action and not someone's wrongdoing. This is a subtle but impactful difference that people will take notice of immediately. It's the difference between creating blame and opening a dialogue.

When you use the word "you," it comes off like you're accusing the person or blaming the listener. Usually, they immediately become defensive almost. People stop listening once they hear the phrase "You did this..." and begin formulating their defense to it.

Focus on your perspective when you're sharing. For example, use "I" statements like "I feel." Frame things as subjective opinion. Tell that person that these are not facts, these are your opinions and you want the opportunity to clarify matters before they get worse. This way, you are lessening the negative impact of what you have to say.

When you position things as opinions that can be changed, then you can get that third story going. You can open the door to that middle-of-the-road compromise that both of you can agree on.

If you start off using the word "you" and you say that "this happened" or "this is a fact", you're making things much harder for yourself. When you approach the difficult conversation as asking the other person for help to clear up an issue, you are inviting a dialogue and inviting a solution. On the other hand, if you are stating that something happened and these are the facts caused by your actions, you're just looking for a fight.

Use cushion phrases like "I hear what you're saying..." or "I never thought of things like that..." or "I had no idea it affected you that way..." You open with acknowledging that what that person has to say is valid and you're letting them know you're listening to them.

This doesn't mean you're compromising your position. All it means is that you are speaking in such a way that you can have a true two-way dialogue instead of immediately starting an argument.

Listen More, Talk Less

The key to being a tactful is to devote more of your time to listening before you talk. Give the other person a chance to feel heard and that their opinion matters. Provide validation, otherwise defensiveness will override all other instincts.

Chapter 7. Tact(ics): Speak To Create A Dialogue

Many people get the wrong idea of what a difficult conversation is.

They just want it to be a catharsis of what they've been holding on their shoulders for weeks or even months. That's part of it, but if that is the primary goal, you are going to have difficulties moving forward and establishing a dialogue.

The hope is ultimately to create a mutually beneficial resolution. Keep this in mind as we go through several more tactics for speaking so people will listen and creating a meaningful dialogue.

Criticism Sandwich

A criticism sandwich is not something you eat.

Instead, it's a powerful technique for communicating an unpleasant fact. For example, if you are a supervisor and you're supposed to give performance review to a subordinate, you can choose one of two options.

You can criticize that person straight out, or you can start off with the positive elements that you saw, discuss the areas for improvement, and then end with a list of other positive attributes. In the former option, you jump right into negativity and you force people into a position of defense. In the latter option, you start off positive to disarm people, gently talk about your concerns, and then end positively so people don't leave with a low sense of self-worth.

Which technique do you think would help the employee feel more empowered?

The criticism sandwich uses positive elements to cushion the blow of matters that may be perceived negatively.

For example, "You're doing great, but if there's one thing... But seriously, you are a rock star and you deserve a promotion!"

Or "I really appreciate how much work you've been doing around the house, but if there's one area I feel a bit confused by, it's concerning the dishes. But seriously, I was so happy when you took care of the car last week, you're so nice."

Keep Emotions at Bay

Negative ones, anyway.

When you're expressing yourself, it's all too easy to show a facial expression or eye roll that completely dissolves your intent and makes the other person feel judged and insulted.

Effective tact eliminates negative emotion and makes it clear that you just want to detail a situation as you saw it and how it impacted you.

You don't want to come off as angry, accusatory, or livid. You have to look at what you're saying as a means of resolving issues. You must have the demeanor of somebody who's out there to ask for help and who is looking to participate in a solution. Your body language has to reflect the same thing.

Microexpressions and other minor body motions might give you away, so it's important to be aware of how you present yourself. Practice what you want to say a few times in front of the mirror and pay special attention to your face. What emotions are you conveying, and is judgment or negativity sneaking through your façade?

Take your pride and ego out of the equation. They will only be detrimental to your goal.

Keep resentment and bitterness out of your voice. Don't raise your voice, yell or speak nervously in a way that implies accusation.

It is actually more favorable to appear robotic than expressive when you're delivering bad news. Keep your canvas clean and let your words deliver the message, not mix signals with your face or body language.

Stick to Facts

As tempting as it may be to use conjecture and assumptions, stick to the facts.

What I mean by this is to never imply things about people, assign intentions to them, or call into question their motivations. You simply don't know these things, so it can be detrimental and borderline insulting to suggest that you do.

Imagine that you have accidentally left your friend's favorite jacket at a restaurant. You call the restaurant later, but it is lost forever. How insulted or annoyed would you be if your friend accused you of losing it intentionally because you've always been jealous of their looks? Or implying that you are always untrustworthy, so they shouldn't have let you handle the jacket at all?

This is accusatory in the worst way and where there was one problem, there are now two: the jacket and their implications of your character.

The positioning of what you're saying should be of collaboration, joint problem solving and asking for help. Even if what you're saying is true, people are often aware of their shortcomings and don't need to hear it from you. Additionally, it invokes their defense mechanisms for their self-esteem, which is a sleeping giant that is best not woken often.

Pay attention to how you normally describe things. If anything smacks of partiality or unfair characterization, it's not going to turn out well for you. Your message will be rejected or people will be skeptical about it.

And besides, if you state an assumption and are instantly shot down as incorrect, your opinion instantly becomes far less credible. This begs the question – *should* they be less credible if there aren't enough facts to support what you are arguing?

Examples and Examples

It's not enough to come to the table with a vague feeling of dissatisfaction.

When you come to someone and say "I don't know, it just doesn't make me feel good!" or "I don't know when, but it just happens a lot," how credible do you think you will appear?

First of all, you might just appear to enjoy whining if you can't back up any of your assertions.

Second, you might appear to be crying out for attention.

Third, you might be seen as overly emotional, and for lack of a better term, a drama queen who wants to create conflict where there isn't.

If you're going to talk to people about negative situations or acts, you need to be prepared with concrete evidence. If there is no concrete evidence of at least two occasions that made you feel the way you do, then provide a clearly explainable path as to how you arrived at that point.

Take a step back.

Do you know why you feel the way you do? Don't involve other people unless you know what you feel and what you want, otherwise you are creating a situation that could be mostly counterproductive.

We're all entitled to our feelings, but the ability to articulate them well is what will make your conversations more productive and effective. If you can't articulate them or provide examples to prove them, then you might just be digging yourself a ditch to sleep in.

Conversations can be scary because they are unpredictable, but the more preparation you do before the fact, the less scary they are. Come in with a blueprint for what you want to bring up with the supporting facts and examples in hand and you won't even have to think about it. You'll know how to approach it instinctually.

Use the Bare Minimum

Difficult conversations require restraint.

This is, of course, because emotions are involved. You feel a catharsis when you unload your suppressed emotions onto someone, so you feel a certain amount of momentum to air everything out, even things that aren't particularly related to the issue at hand.

But too much is sometimes... well, too much. There's only a finite amount of punishment one can take in one day, whether it is justified or not.

So get in and get out with what you have to say. The more you meander around the topic or beat the horse dead, the more unnecessary it becomes. If you've already made the impact and conveyed the message you wanted, then it's time to stop.

There is a point of diminishing returns – in other words, if you end up unloading everything onto them, the less effective the important points will be. They will be hidden and obscured, and you will overwhelm the listener with your seemingly extraneous negativity.

Focus on the bare minimum that you need to say to clearly convey your point. Keep the negativity there only. You don't have to be so blunt that it comes off that you're intending it to hurt. Focus instead on a short, compact way to say what you need to say that doesn't step on the emotional toes of the person that you're conversing with.

Ask yourself: *What is the purpose of what I am about to say? Will it do more to fulfill my purpose and goal, or is it actually just to inflict pain on the other person?*

Are you adding more negativity tinder because it makes you feel good to get revenge or observe someone's pain?

Focus only on what you need to say so it pushes the conversation forward and hopefully opens the door to resolution. Anything else can either be misunderstood or subconsciously used to flat out hurt the other person. Speak your message and get out – rest assured that there *was* impact.

Chapter 8. Choose Your Battles

Choosing your battles is something that some parents, namely overbearing parents, could have learned.

For some of us, it seemed like they never gave us a break. Every other sentence was some form of nagging where we had to improve or stop performing poorly. It was constant and never ending.

In other words, some parents never chose their battles. They seem like they want 100% of everything, all the time. This is, of course, understandable, because very few people will ever feel a parental instinct towards us besides our own parents.

However, when we're going through the constant, non-stop nagging and arguments, it's exhausting. The typical response to this is to tune them out entirely, decide that they are making a mountain out of a molehill, and stop listening completely.

It's the case of the boy who cried wolf. If you can't choose your battles for when to engage in a difficult conversation, people will stop taking you seriously and listening to what you have to say.

It is typically only years later when we reach far into adulthood that we realize the knowledge of what our parents were saying. Do you want this to be the case for you and the recipient of your difficult conversation?

It's easy to react to everything that displeases you or rubs you the wrong way. But if you were to do that, nothing would ever get done, and you would very quickly be labeled as a contentious malcontent. And the thing is, people wouldn't be wrong.

At best, you would be perceived as very annoying, and at worst, a total waste of time to speak with. Just as bad, both parties will grow exhausted. Save your time and energy by choosing your battles wisely.

If you're reading this book, you're probably bursting at the seams with a difficult conversation you want to address immediately. Here are a few guiding questions to determine whether you need to be more conscious in choosing your battles and engaging.

Is This Necessary Now?

Ask yourself: Is this topic necessary now?

Difficult conversations can either involve immediate resolutions or open the door for future resolution. These are equally valuable. Don't think that you have to pack all the issues you have and handle them in the here and now.

To do things that way might kick up a lot of dust and both parties might end up overreacting.

Look at the grand scheme of things and figure out which issues can you work on now and use these to lay the groundwork for further discussions in the future.

Does it really matter all that much, or is it part of a pattern? Are there long-term implications or is this just a one-time thing? Is there a possibility that it would balloon out of control at some point if you talk about it now?

You have to weigh these different considerations carefully. They play a big role in whether you should talk about that particular topic or gradually open the person up to discussing those topics later.

Another "now?" question to answer is your mood. Is your negative mood blowing things out of proportion? Are you really just tired and cranky from not sleeping the night before? What would an objective third party say about what transpired? Are you looking at things in a calm and objective manner or are you so emotionally worked up that things seem to be more dramatic than they need to be?

The bottom line is that not all the problems that you're thinking of addressing are worth dealing with right now. They're not really all that important.

Have you ever seen a news story where someone gets stabbed over a traffic disagreement or over who gets the last piece of pizza?

It's not the piece of pizza they're fighting over. They are fighting over their emotions which have ballooned out of control unnecessarily. As I said in the beginning of the chapter, are you choosing to turn everything into a battle?

Cooling Periods

A cooling period is a period of inaction. It's a time where you think about what happened, and where you are driven less by emotion and more by objective logic.

What happened, was it intentional, what's the harm, and how do I truly feel about it?

This means that in the face of anything potentially enraging, put yourself into a short cooling period, or time out, to drift back down to earth. Yes, just like an angry toddler throwing a tantrum. I have no trouble characterizing myself as one at times.

You are entitled to your emotions, but do yourself a big favor and wait about fifteen minutes so that they aren't taken out on the other person. This will enable you to think more clearly about how they may respond as well as their actions and what their intentions were.

In addition to the 15-minute rule, I stick with the rule of three.

One offending act is acceptable as a lack of foresight or ignorance. Two becomes a borderline area where I am cautious, yet still say nothing in the possibility of incidental action.

The third time is when I start to give less benefit of the doubt and engage in a difficult conversation. This simple rule also helps insert a lot of calming time between the infractions and engaging with the person.

Point of No Return

When choosing your battles, it's helpful to establish a point of no return, or a dealbreaker. This is a personal line in the sand that cannot be crossed for you. It is a non-negotiable that will trigger serious action.

What's an example of this? Making a joke about a deceased relative. You get the idea.

The line you choose to create is a boundary as to how respected you feel. Crossing it constitutes a serious insult, so choose its location carefully.

Consider the Costs

Remember, the moment you decide to call somebody out and have a difficult conversation, tension is created.

Even if you're right and even if you know that you will win, there will be a trade-off. Your relationship might not be the same ever again. There may be tension established in your workspace that will take forever to resolve.

This is one of the main reasons that people hate confrontation in the first place. People will proclaim "It will be awkward!" or "We have to see each other too much!"

They're not wrong, and that's why it is doubly important to choose your battles based on their value, and not the principle. When will the benefits (value) outweigh the costs? At what point will it be worth the tradeoff?

In some situations, letting go is far more effective than a difficult conversation ever will be.

Chapter 9. Create Safety

Suppose you have a friend that you tell your dating stories to.

He or she fails to see the humor in your failed dates, and furthermore, doesn't think that pre-marital dating should exist in any form. He or she believes that you should marry the first person you kiss.

When he or she makes these beliefs apparent to you, do you think you're going to keep telling him or her your dating stories? No chance.

You'd stop immediately because you would know that with every sentence, your friend is judging you and mentally labeling you. They've eliminated the space for you to be vulnerable and you don't feel safe sharing with them anymore.

The same situation plays out with difficult conversations. In order for people to open up to you, or you to them, there must be a sphere of safety wherein the parties don't feel judged for expressing their thoughts or emotions. They need to be able to let their guard down for extended periods of time, and they won't do that unless there is guaranteed safety.

If you're not extremely careful in how you choose your words and how you position your stance, it's easy to look like you're judging them. It's easy to come off as accusatory and not open to their perspective.

At the first sign of judgment, you'll be met with either a blank wall or evasive defensiveness. That's what happens when people know there is a negative result upcoming and they want to avoid it. What lies ahead are methods to create comfort and above all else, the safety in a difficult conversation that will allow it to move forward without negative backlash.

Set up the conversation such that people feel safe enough to participate in it.

Divulge First

People are often insecure about what they're feeling inside. In many cases, they may think that whatever they're feeling may not be valid.

A great way to counteract this common feeling is to be the first one to reveal something that puts you in a negative light or in a compromising position. Be the first person to share something that is potentially embarrassing and make yourself vulnerable.

This sets the tone with the person you are trying to

confront. You are demonstrating to them that it's okay to be vulnerable. If I can do it, then you can too.

There will be a feeling of genuine trust because you've entrusted them with something about yourself. People will usually reciprocate and feel comfortable because you are theoretically not in a position to judge.

For example, if you wanted someone to open up about how they feel neglected, you might share an anecdote where you hated feeling neglected by an ex because it made you feel so worthless. They might just agree with you when they see that you understand their perspective.

No Position to Judge

Always remember that judgment has no place in a difficult conversation because it will kill it quickly.

The best way to wrap your mind around this is to think about how you felt when people judged you unfairly in the past. Maybe people talked behind your back and came to some unfair conclusions. Whatever the case, they made some negative assumptions about you.

How does that feel? Now, remember that feeling because you don't want to make other people feel that.

If you can step into their shoes as the recipient of judgment, then this should open your mind to actively guarding against a judgmental tone. The bottom line is that you are no better than anyone else, so you are in no position to judge.

Judgment has the side effect of feeding into negativity, putting an overtone of criticism and displeasure over the entire conversation.

Difficult conversations are not about making moral judgments. They are about resolving issues.

Create Safety

As long as the following conditions are present, you can create a space where people can feel vulnerable without feeling insecure and judged.

Don't interrupt people's thoughts. Do not talk over them. Let them say their piece. If you interrupt people, you're essentially commenting that what they are feeling is invalid and it's incredibly frustrating to be cut off mid-thought. This can make them feel very defensive very quickly.

Don't outright refute what they have to say. Don't say, "You're wrong" even if that's what you want to scream. Don't say "Maybe what you're feeling is not really what you're feeling." When you refute or rebut what they say, this invalidates their feelings. Always acknowledge first, especially in the heat of the moment. Don't lead with "No."

Avoid filling in the silences. They're not waiting for you to reply, they're thinking about what else they want to divulge to you. People are trying to get their thoughts together. They're trying to decide what they're going to say next. They're also trying to sort certain things that are flashing through their minds. Give them the time and space to completely speak their thoughts.

Let them figure things out and then say it. Don't try to prod them. Don't try to fill in the gaps that they've left. Don't make them feel pressured and harassed. Respect these silences when necessary.

Stress the importance of non-judgment and remind all participants in the conversation that your goal is to solve a problem. Your goal is not to find blame. Your goal is not to judge people or make them feel uncomfortable. Your goal is to facilitate some sort of resolution. This creates a safe space because people will feel that their feedback is necessary to solve the problem at hand.

Ask questions motivated by genuine curiosity and emphasize that motivation. Do not ask loaded questions such as "You ate all the pie just because you wanted to see me angry, didn't you?" Do not ask questions where you imply certain judgments. This is not an argument. You're engaged in this difficult conversation because you want to resolve issues. You're trying to help each other.

When you use loaded questions or leading questions, it's too easy for the recipient to conclude that you're there to judge them or you have some sort of hidden agenda. You imply you're not really there to solve the issue. You're there to make them feel bad, or accuse them, or blame them.

Never draw conclusions. When you talk, don't say, "So, this is what happens. This is what you're feeling." You see, people own their feelings and thoughts. You can't step into their shoes. You can't see what they see. You can't feel what they feel. When you make conclusions about these things you are judging them. You are essentially overriding or invalidating their right to their own feelings and thoughts.

Finally, when you are trying to create a safe space, make sure that your facial expressions are neutral and empathetic. Don't show disdain or displeasure. Don't roll your eyes, scoff, or shake your head. Remember, your goal is to facilitate resolution. Your goal is to solve a problem – not to judge, pick sides, and definitely not to blame.

Chapter 10: Be Solution-Oriented

I've implied and talked about this in previous chapters, but not stated it outright.

You have to remember that your overall goal here is to come up with a solution. Does this mean that all difficult discussions will always lead to a happy resolution for both parties? Of course not, but by having a solution-oriented approach, you are putting yourself in a more favorable spot for the situation to never repeat itself. You are positioning yourself in such a way that the conversation will lead to a more positive place.

When you are solution oriented, you are looking to take action and remedy the underlying situation ahead. You are looking for root causes and you're looking to collaborate. You want to come out of your conversation with specific steps to take action with for maximum effectiveness.

This is very different from being problem oriented. When you're problem oriented, you're looking for the problems and examining the aftereffects. You're looking backwards, where being solution oriented looks forward.

Which do you think is solution oriented and problem oriented? "Why did the problem cause such a big mess?" and "How do I figure out the problem in my path?" If you're still a bit fuzzy on this, the solution-oriented approach is the second question. One approach focuses on the roadblock, while the other focuses on how to circumvent it.

Solutions Beget Success

If you are successful in any area of life, it's because you've looked for and found solutions. You don't rise to the top of any field, or improve yourself, by standing in front of problems and bemoaning them. To overcome them you've taken responsibility, thought clearly, and worked to resourcefully move to the next level.

It's a mindset of looking into the future at the result you want, and working backwards to how you will get there from that roadblock in front of you.

Solution-oriented people don't run away from an ugly truth. They're willing to stare it in the eye and take responsibility, take ownership of the situation, and work collaboratively, so that they don't have to make the same mistake again.

Solution-oriented people also don't get stuck in the "I don't know" zone. They are willing to explore their options. Instead, they're exploring alternative solutions and sorting through different priorities. This is why they're able to stay calm in the midst of chaos – they are already working on the key to overcoming the chaos.

While everybody else is running around like chickens with their heads cut off, solution-oriented people are able to look at the situation objectively, then trying to piece together an idea of what the end result should look like. They look at the goal and then step away from it to try to piece together implementations towards those end objectives.

Some call it "hustle" and others call it "grit." The end result is just someone who achieves their goals and objectives no matter their state of mind.

Establish a Framework

Just like you might approach any other type of problem with a plan of attack, you need one for interpersonal conflict as well.

Here's what you need to focus on:

- What happened?
- Why did it happen?
- What led to it happening?
- What do both parties want?
- How can we give them both what they want?
- What are three ways each party can get what they want?
- Will this prevent similar occurrences in the future?

The most important part of this framework is to come away with three items for each party to think about to improve the situation. When you realize that there are many ways to reach an amicable solution, you will further think creatively and solve issues outside of the box.

Don't focus on what *is*, focus on what *can be*.

It's too easy to just focus on the way things currently are and feel stuck. Solution-oriented people rarely feel stuck because they're always looking at what could be. They have no problems thinking outside the box. As a solution-oriented person, you don't entertain thoughts of assigning blame, finding fault, or listing out things that should have happened. You just focus on the way things already are and look for the logical way out.

<u>Know What You Want</u>

Know what you want out of the difficult conversation. Know what your ideal outcome is and what you want to accomplish overall. Know what you are working towards because that can influence everything you say.

Stay realistic. Generate your ideal outcome with alternatives that reflect context and the human element. Lay it out at the beginning so others know what you want with no hidden agendas.

Be flexible and ready to adapt and change. In many cases, ideal outcomes only appear when the situation is right.

Don't insist that there is only one ideal resolution to your difficult conversation. You're simply just painting yourself into a corner, and working yourself up emotionally, when others don't agree with your sole vision.

For example, you might take issue with how someone is treating your property with little respect. How do you approach this being solution-oriented?

You know your goal is to make sure that your property isn't damaged. The ideal outcome is for them to outright admit that they are being rude and buy you a new version of everything they've scuffed or scratched. This is not likely to happen.

There's no sense in fixating on the damage itself. It is already done and in the past. How can you move forward to a damage-free world?

Following the framework, what were the conditions surrounding the property damage and how can you formulate a solution to make sure it doesn't happen again? What are you doing to contribute to their negligence?

Solutions beget success so it only makes sense to focus on them. Otherwise, talking about the same problem over and over can quickly become a waste of time and life.

Chapter 11. The Five Phases To Difficult Conversations

Just like with any story, there's a beginning, middle, and end to a difficult conversation.

There are certain phases and a definite sequence to follow to ensure that you achieve your goals and incorporate all of what I've talked about in earlier chapters of the book. Certain phases paint the details for the subsequent steps and need to be introduced before other details are brought out.

Following the sequence as a natural process makes the mountain of a difficult conversation easy. You don't have to think about what to talk about next, and you don't have to reinvent the wheel in the heat of a tense moment.

It also makes sure that you touch upon everything that you need to make others feel safe, comfortable, validated, and heard.

This is the chapter where we put all that I have described so far together and dive into a real difficult conversation. Most difficult conversations are not about huge issues; rather, they involve the accumulation of daily tension. You know what I'm talking about: from not cleaning the dishes, to talking too much about yourself, to not picking up the dirty socks from the floor.

These are problems just like any others that require resolution.

Recalling that in a previous chapter I stated that there is no perfect time to begin a difficult conversation, the first phase is to break the ice.

Phase One: Breaking the Ice

People don't like to have difficult conversations and they will go to great lengths to avoid them. They will avoid people and locations, and stray from their regular patterns just to not see someone.

In a sense, breaking the ice will be like trying to catch a slippery eel. You may have something you want to say, but people won't give you an opening to say it.

That's why it's important to be clear and direct at the outset of a difficult conversation. Right when you meet with someone or arrange a meeting, tell them that you want to talk about something. Don't lure them there under the pretense that it's just a friendly catch- up session. Don't bait and switch them.

This prepares you, but also prepares them to think about what has transpired and what they think about it. There is no sweeping it under the rug, so they'll have to confront you.

You can set the stage in a very casual way by simply saying, "Hey, we need to talk." It doesn't really matter what you say because the impact will be there regardless of how you phrase it. Their guards will be slightly up, but that's worth it to ensure that they don't keep avoiding you.

As I've mentioned in a previous chapter, you need to pick your battles very carefully. Make sure that what you're about to talk about is truly important. Think hard about the long-term implications of having this difficult conversation. Your relationship might suffer permanently because of the talk you're about to get into, even if you do everything correctly and tactfully. Be certain that you are resorting to this step because you need to.

Break the ice to set up a comfort level. From the beginning you have to make it clear to the person through your body language, facial expression, verbal and nonverbal communications that he or she is in ally. You're looking for that person to contribute to a joint solution.

You have to make it clear to that person that they are not a problem you're trying to solve. You definitely don't want to imply that you're blaming or condemning them at some level or other. By looking to collaborate and work together, and setting the tone of your discussion to reflect that, you break the ice the right way.

Phase Two: Your Issues

This is the phase where most people fall short or damage

the potential of a difficult conversation.

After you set a meeting where there is clear intent to discuss something difficult, there's no sense in engaging in small talk. After both parties sit down, this is your time to discuss what's been weighing on your chest.

Implore them to not interrupt because you'll keep it short.

You want to be the first to speak because you set the tone for how the conversation will go, and if you follow the steps in this chapter, it will result in a collaborative and peaceful tone. Speaking first also allows you to air your grievances in a way that frames fault on both parties, where the other person might not see it that way. Being the first to admit fault is a powerful ingredient in having people be amenable to what you're saying.

However, you must do this so that the other person doesn't feel instantly attacked and lambasted.

Resist the temptation of bringing out a long laundry list of issues that you have with that person. This is not the appropriate time for that and doesn't necessarily advance your overall goal. Focus primarily on what needs to be resolved. Keep your list of issues short, compact, and direct to the point.

Try not to talk about these issues in a long, drawn out way. The more you beat around the bush, the higher the likelihood that you're going to send signals that you are insulting the person, judging the other party, and otherwise making things harder for yourself. It's too easy to step on these common landmines when you're talking about delicate topics.

First, separate intent from impact.

Make it clear to that person you're not judging their intent and that anything they were at fault for was an accident.

The ongoing example for this chapter is a hypothetical conversation about housekeeping duties. separating intent from impact in this example is when you state up front, "I know you don't intend to make the house dirty and you like it clean, too."

This sentence communicates clearly to the person that you view them as an ally. You view that person as a contributor to a clean house. You make it clear to them that both of you share the same desire and value for clean surroundings. This means there must be a misunderstanding somewhere because you two have the same intentions.

Second, focus on the cause and not the symptoms.

Focus on why certain patterns happen again and again. A great way to phrase this in the house cleanliness example is to say, "I've just been trying to figure out why this is happening because I thought we were always on the same page. Maybe you have been really tired at work lately and just don't have the time to clean up? I totally know how that feels."

The phrasing doesn't focus on that person intending to make the house dirty or that person being somehow or in some way a slob. Instead, it traces the problem behavior to something more neutral like being tired from work.

The third step is to employ tactful "I" statements.

This really is a way of turning the statements you'd rather say as "you" statements into a less offensive form. For example, you can say, "I feel like I work hard to keep the house clean, but lately it's been below the level I like."

This highlights your perspective, your feelings, and the reality that you perceive, but presents it in an inoffensive way. You then quickly back out the "I" statements with specific examples.

This is crucial. You can't just end the conversation based on how you feel. Maybe the way you're feeling is not based on reality. Maybe there's no concrete evidence that led to your conclusion. Maybe your conclusion is faulty.

You can say, "For example, the downstairs living room is scattered with your things, so I'm just confused."

Make sure that you present a quizzical or confused impression. that's how someone feels when they are facing a problem to solve, not accusing someone. It also shows that you aren't angry, just confused.

Phase Three: Their Response

Now that you've laid out your problems, the next step is to listen to the other party's response.

You don't do this by simply sitting there and nodding your head, however. You need to create a safe space for vulnerability, encourage them to open up, and diffuse defensiveness.

You have to anticipate that they will be defensive and feel put on the spot.

You can neutralize this by saying certain things to create a space for shared vulnerability and being the first to admit fault. For example, "I know that I sometimes forget to clean up, sometimes I'm just so busy I don't even shower or brush my teeth. I just want to figure out how to keep both of us happy."

You claim part of the blame. You claim, "It's not all you, sometimes I screw up as well." You also give them an opening for owing up to their part of the situation.

The second element to effective listening is to supply emotional and logical validation. A great example of this would be to say, "I understand how it is to be so tired and stressed at work. I hear you. Of course, you had no choice to let go a little around the house. I do the same every couple of weeks. It makes sense."

When you do this, you let them know that you get what they're going through, but this doesn't make the objective reality of the messy house go away. All this does is create a safe space so you can have a mature, and hopefully, productive conversation regarding how the both of you can work together to solve the issue.

of course, don't interrupt, let them fill silences, and keep neutral facial expressions to encourage them to speak.

Listening isn't the easy part – it's the tough part where you find out what really matters. It is by no means passive. In general, summarize what they say back to them so you know you are on the same page. They will either confirm or correct you and elaborate further.

Don't give advice or offer solutions until the next phase.

Phase Four: Find the Third Story

Once you have created a safe space and you have listened to that other person's response, everything is laid out on the table.

Each side has their own story, and it's up to you both to work together like Sherlock Holmes and Watson to find the third story.

An example of this is to say, "So the real story is that I thought you were mad at me and being messy on purpose, but you were just stressed out from the big project at work, so you didn't have time."

It reminds everybody involved that, "Hey, we're in the same boat together and we're trying to solve a problem. There's no bad guy here. We're trying to come to a solution that works for both of us."

Once you find it, create the middle-of-the-road solution or compromise that would make both participants feel that they're walking away a winner.

Phase Five: Solution Orientation

After you've discovered the third story, or at least an explanation that appears reasonable to both parties, you need to be called to action.

"How do we go forward and make sure that something like this doesn't happen again,?"

Each party should generate a list of suggestions on things they personally can do in the future to remedy the situation or keep it from happening.

For example, you might be more focused on letting your standards of cleanliness slip a little, and the other person might be more focused on hiring a maid for when they are particularly tired.

This puts them on notice as to what's expected to change and as to what is expected of them.

Warning

Make sure that you follow all the phases above in a face-to-face discussion.

Never do it over email. Never do it over the phone. This has to be handled on a face-to-face basis because you're constantly giving off nonverbal and verbal signals to the person you're speaking to. A lot of crucial facial expressions, tone of voice, and other signals cannot be detected when you're communicating with somebody over text messages, email, or online chat.

What happens when you get into an argument with someone over the Internet? It's a disaster, without fail, even if you win decisively.

As much as possible, try to do it when you're both physically in front of each other.

Chapter 12. Feedback With Grace

If you've ever had a boss, chances are that you've had a performance review.

Performance reviews are never 100% positive, so how did you feel about the feedback and criticism you were given?

It can either energize and excite you for the next opportunity to perform better, or it can demoralize you and destroy your self-esteem.

Giving feedback, whether it's positive or negative, is often a difficult conversation in and of itself. This is because the possibility for confrontation and bruised egos is often lurking nearby, so people step on eggshells and generally avoid the situation as best they can.

Feedback isn't just about job performance or how well your last speech was received, it also exists in the context of a difficult conversation. It's a debriefing afterwards that makes people feel better after inevitable tension and that the relationship won't be altered for the worse.

Don't skip the feedback portion of a difficult conversation. Use phrases such as "I'm really glad we talked about this. I felt like you might be defensive, but you weren't. I know I got a little mad and thanks for dealing with that. I'm glad we worked on our three action items and can move past this." It's easy to lose the spirit of the conversation and whatever resolutions for change were made.

It's the final period to a difficult conversation. Whatever the context, here are some invaluable methods to approach giving feedback, especially negative criticism, with grace and peace.

What's the Purpose?

The point of giving feedback must be positive. It must all be about growth, helping someone fix or improve something, and prevent further issues from flaring up.

It's not about correcting the other person or putting them in their place. It's not about talking over the other person or trying to verbally dominate them. In short, when you give feedback, you're not trying to rebut a debating partner. You're looking to help someone on their journey to happiness, productivity, or whatever might be their end goal.

Effective feedback can build confidence and alert people to their blind spots. These are force multipliers that can take them to the next level, often with you to credit.

which part is you venting about someone (to their face, and for the purpose of making you feel better), and which part is actually going to help them? Again, it's a case of choosing your battles carefully so people don't tune you out.

Safety

Check back to Chapter 9 where I covered creating a safe space so people can display vulnerability in front of you.

It's really important to create a safe space when you're giving feedback. Remember to let the person you're speaking with know that you're not judging their character just because you are telling them something negative. It doesn't reflect on them as a person just because they're not good at doing the dishes. State this explicitly.

If people feel that whatever they're going to say is going to be rejected, ridiculed, or otherwise marginalized, they will quickly conclude that there's really no point to receiving your feedback. You have to take the initiative to make it clear that when people give feedback you're not going to judge them. You're not going to use it as an opportunity to launch an attack on that other person.

Specificity

When you give feedback, it needs specific details for credibility.

Give detailed examples of the behavior or actions in question, otherwise it's just a vague feeling you have about something that you can't articulate.

Give detailed statements about your emotional state and

how it was affected by their actions or what they said.

However, it's important to note that if you've made a point earlier in the discussion, don't use the feedback process to hammer that point endlessly. If you've already made your point, you should filter yourself to prevent yourself from going overboard. At that point, you're speaking for yourself and just adding tension to an already tense situation.

By simply repeating a negative point in the feedback process, you are going to make the person you're talking with suspicious about your motives. This can put the person on the spot and instead of creating a safe space where you can exchange feedback in a nonjudgmental way, they can't help but conclude that you're judging or condemning them.

Use the Losada Ratio

According to the Losada Ratio, named after Dr. Marcial Losada, researchers have discovered that there is an optimal ratio between positive and negative comments to ensure productivity in any difficult discussion. People tune out and their defense mechanisms rise too high after too much repeated negativity.

According to the researchers, you need to mention three positive comments for every item of negative feedback for an optimal outcome in your conversation.

If all your feedback is negative, it will poison the feedback process and whatever gains you've achieved in the discussion will disappear.

Pay close attention to the Losada Ratio. Pay attention to the words coming out of your mouth, think before you talk and try to stick to the ratio. Avoid the temptation of hammering home the same negative points that you've already mentioned. If you've already made a negative point earlier, there's no point in repeating it.

Use Collaborative Words

There are certain words that bring people together like "and" and "what if" and "what do you think about…"?

For example, "What if we tried it this way for the next month to see if it improves?"

These work better than "but" and "however" in allowing people to get on the soap box and just simply let the juices flow without fear that they would be judged.

For example, "I like that way, however, it's not the most effective use of your time."

As unavoidable as the words "but" or "however" might be, try to temper their effect by using words and phrases that draw both you and the other party together. The whole point of watching the words that you use is to subtly suggest a collaborative process rather than an adversarial process. Even if you want to completely change something overnight, you have to mold the conversation so you don't put the other party off.

Receive Well

When it's the other party's turn to give feedback, don't interrupt them. This will make you appear closed-minded and defensive. It takes courage for them to talk to you in this manner, so appreciate it and let them carry on.

Listen intently and do not justify your actions or lay out evidence to the contrary until they are done.

Your goal is to maintain a comfortable and accepting space between you and the person you're speaking with. By getting defensive, you shrink that space quickly.

In many cases, people automatically read into certain statements the worst possible interpretation. In many cases, people end up arguing over and over about what the other person said, when it turns out that the other person actually said something fairly neutral or obvious that was not really that offensive.

By being too eager to jump in and interpret the feedback in the worst way possible, you run the risk of destroying your exchange.

Just listen at first and take it all in. Ask questions for the purpose of clarifying exactly what they meant and what they considered the problem to be. After all, even if you're on the receiving end, there is still a problem to be solved together.

Chapter 13. Know BATNA And WATNA

The terms BATNA and WATNA are terms that you'll only hear from an experienced negotiator's mouth.

As in, "What's our BATNA or WATNA if this talk doesn't work out?"

BATNA stands for the Best Alternative To a Negotiated Agreement.

In other words, if you avoid a difficult conversation, or it falls flat on its face, what's the best case scenario? For example, the best offer to sell your car you have is for $1,000 USD. If you don't have a difficult conversation about selling your car, then your BATNA is $1,000 USD. That's the best offer you'll get if things fail or go south. It's your ideal safety net, so to speak.

Alternatively, WATNA stands for the Worst Alternative To a Negotiated Agreement.

In other words, if your difficult conversation goes south and fails utterly, what's the worst case scenario? In the example above, the best offer to sell your car was for $1,000 USD. That was the most you were going to get in the situation if the difficult conversation went poorly.

What's the worst you'll get in the situation if the conversation goes poorly? Nothing. Zero. Zilch.

The WATNA here is if the $1,000 USD offer disappears or changes their mind. You get nothing for the car – though you still have the car and have to broker further deals. That is not taken into account in the BATNA and WATNA because your goal is to not keep the car.

Just to recap, the BATNA and WATNA come into play when you are considering your choices on whether or not to have a difficult conversation.

If you want to have a difficult conversation, you must realize what's waiting for you should you choose to walk away from it – the best version and the worst version.

Consider this a more nuanced method of choosing your battles and deciding where to draw your line in the sand.

It's important to keep BATNA and WATNA in mind because they give you some sort of system for weighing all the pros and cons of engaging difficult conversations in the first place.

If your conversation fails or blows up in your face, or the desired effect is not reached, you then have to ask yourself if you can live with the BATNA. Alternatively, are you prepared for the WATNA? How urgent does this make your conversation?

Let's take an example from before: where you wish to confront your roommate or significant other about cleanliness in the shared household.

What is your BATNA and WATNA should the difficult conversation explode in your face?

The best case scenario you can hope for is that your roommate or significant other eventually realizes they are wrong and cleans up their act on their own. This isn't a very good best case scenario, however, because it depends on them changing on their own and without outside influences. Another potential BATNA might be that, should the difficult conversation about cleaning go poorly, you talk to their friend about it and they eventually win your roommate over.

Neither scenario is great.

What's the WATNA – the worst case scenario if your difficult conversation about cleaning goes poorly?

Pretty bad, actually. If the conversation goes poorly, the worst case scenario is a tense and angry household filled with passive-aggression. Your roommate may feel attacked and victimized, and they will act out against you. They'll also feel disrespected and diminished.

So can you live with the BATNA and are you prepared for the WATNA?

You must balance the BATNA and WATNA against what you can gain if the difficult conversation goes off without a hitch.

This is a great way of wrapping your mind clearly and effectively around the pros and cons of difficult conversations. You might be emotionally prepared and you might think that having that conversation makes all the sense in the world, but if you run it through the BATNA and WATNA filter, it might turn out that if things go badly, you end up losing more than you're prepared for.

If anything, the BATNA and WATNA filter, and thinking process, enables you to get a clear picture of what's at stake in your decision to have or not have a difficult conversation.

In addition to discussing very hard topics with people close to you or people at work, BATNA and WATNA can also help you with practical negotiations. It gives you probabilities as to outcomes to think about, so you can shape your negotiation position properly. At the very least, thinking about your negotiation in terms of BATNA and WATNA enables you to decide how hard to push for certain points and determine outcomes that you can or cannot live with.

Chapter 14. Negotiation Tactics

At first glance, negotiations and difficult conversations don't share many similarities. One happens in the context of perhaps determining an employee's salary, and the other happens in the context of confronting someone over hurt feelings.

However, the superficial similarities eventually show themselves. They can both be emotionally taxing. They can be intense. They also require you to have a clear idea of what your main points are.

The deeper similarities soon become apparent. Both situations inherently involve tension and working together towards a common solution that both parties feel good about.

They are basically the same situation, except negotiation is by nature much more adversarial. In most people's minds, for them to gain, the other party has to lose something.

But that's only if you approach negotiation as a static pie that can't be enlarged or changed to another flavor. The best way to approach a negotiation is to create multiple pies so that everyone can have the amount of pie they want to create a win-win situation.

Tip One: Speak First

In any negotiation or difficult conversation (as shown by the five phases in Chapter 11), it's beneficial to speak first so you can set the tone as non-adversarial as possible. You are also able to anchor the values of what you want and what you are going to be negotiating about.

For example, if you lead with an offer of $100 USD, then you force the other person to adapt and react to that price. They can't suddenly shift to the opening offer of $50 that they were originally going to make.

By simply laying things out, you mentally condition the other party to the range of possible actions they can take regarding the deal. This sets you to set the tone and lay out your objections and points so they are on the defensive.

Finally, being the first to speak allows you to position the conversation based on what matters to you. People often buy and sell stuff or negotiate certain deals due to different concerns. If you're looking for a new home as opposed to a used home, you can position the negotiation so that considerations regarding the condition are put front and center.

Tip Two: People Want Other Things

This is one of the most important principles in any

negotiation. People often want other things than what they have presented, so it's up to you to find those things.

Once you can tap into their true desires, you truly enlarge the aforementioned pie because you aren't fighting over the same real estate anymore.

For example, suppose you want to sell a car. You might think that your primary objective is to get money for the car so you can put that towards a new car. However, the buyer might offer you less money, but combined with a dealership membership and services that would be beneficial for a new car owner. You would take less money overall, but possibly get more value for yourself.

People want things that they don't realize sometimes.

You are able to create a win-win situation where the buyer pays less money and provides services that are of no cost to them, but of great value to you. Both parties get more of what they want, and give up less than they thought they would. If it sounds like each party is trading up, they usually are.

The secret is to step into the shoes of the party you're negotiating with and look at the range of benefits they would want from a deal.

Is someone's primary objective simply money, or is there something else they would be happy with in lieu of money? What is their end goal and how can you more directly affect that? Coincidentally, these may be things you are more willing to give up.

If someone is selling a car, like above, you have to think about why they are selling the car and what they hope to achieve. Money, convenience, a tax break, lower overhead costs, increase storage space, reduce waste, and so on. On a secondary level, you can think about what a person intends to do with the money they get from selling their car and appeal to that motive.

By understanding the priorities of each party's objectives, you can set things up so you get what you want and they get what they want, and everybody walks away feeling like a winner.

By thinking outside the box and focusing on where your interests overlap and where other interests lay you create a situation where you can produce a win-win deal.

Tip Three: Be the First to Address Your Flaws

No matter how solid you think your position is, your opponent can always find something to criticize and nitpick. These small things are sometimes allowed to snowball into dealbreakers, so it's important for you to address them.

You need to be the first to bring them up, lay them out, address them, then refute them.

Don't wait for the other party to raise it, because you want to anchor the other party's perspective on the issue. Take their biggest piece of ammunition and use it for yourself. You will disarm them and catch them off guard. Show them you are aware of their thought process and are one step ahead. Show your awareness and logical mind. Display honesty and courage.

"Now, I know what you are going to say about my plan. They'll say it's unreasonable and illogical. But here's why they're wrong, and the research to back it up."

Objectively talk about your flaw, and do it in an honest way where you aren't minimizing the flaw. Then lay it out and address everything on your terms before they approach it in unfavorable and unreasonable terms.

Often, this will make the other party panic because you've minimized your weakness and emphasized your strengths. You've left them more vulnerable and this can, if positioned properly, open their minds to compromised solutions that ensure you get what you're looking for.

Tip Four: Use Objective Standards

Whenever possible, base your arguments and stances on facts, statistics, and other objective verifiable data.

Arguing based on opinion and emotion has a place and time, but it's only as a topper to when there is an objective basis to what you're saying. Anybody can come up with an opinionated argumentation.

For example, if you're selling your car and asking for a certain price, it's better if you can justify it based on what other similar cars have sold for in the area. That should be your starting point and floor.

However, it's not just for instances like that. The more facts, standards, and statistics you can utilize, the more credible and authoritative you become on your negotiation. If you are able to make this case, your arguments look more ironclad. It's harder for the other party to attack it from a purely subjective basis because they'd also have to come up with objective facts, statistics, and third party standards to substantiate their rebuttal.

Knowing the objective standards also allows you to know exactly when you should walk away and cut your losses, so to speak.

If you want to sell your car and you don't receive any offers for half the objective price, then it's to your benefit to walk away for the time being, and you know this from an objective perspective. You know for a fact you can do better later.

Tip Five: Focus on Pressure

The other side is negotiating with you because somehow or some way they're feeling some compelling pressure to make a deal.

If this wasn't the case, very rarely would they be negotiating with you. If you can recognize this and pinpoint the specific pressure that someone is facing, you can open up an avenue to emphasize.

For example, if it is a known fact that what you have is scarce or dwindling in supply, the other side is on tremendous pressure to buy what you have because chances are good they cannot buy it anywhere else. The demand has just risen while the supply has shrunk.

Similarly, if you know that someone is under pressure to sell a car because they need money to pay back their brother-in-law, then you would emphasize that pressure by bringing up how much family discord would be caused and how much trust would be lost within the family.

The general theme in this chapter is to always attempt to find the prime or secondary motivator for the other party. Here's a hint: it's not always what you think it is.

That's how you enlarge the pie to make a win-win situation. Whatever value you possess can be doubled or tripled if you know exactly what someone wants from a negotiation or situation.

Chapter 15. Dealing With Impossible People

Everything I've presented in this book thus far has been the result of either years of personal experience, or peer-validated psychological research.

And despite that, sometimes none of the tactics described will work. It's a stretch to assume that everyone can be reasoned with and swayed by logic, and it would be detrimental to rely on it.

As you no doubt know, some people can be hands down *impossible*.

Take, for example, a man I recently met abroad who possessed the single worst trait a human can have – they need to be seen as an expert in *everything* and can't stand being wrong.

It's a human trait that we all fall victim to at times, so it's not that some people are impossible. We are all impossible given the right set of circumstances and triggers.

When that happens, it's like speaking to a wall. Regardless

of what you say and how you appeal to facts, sound reasoning, and logic, nothing seems to work. They're simply ignoring whatever you're saying and tuning you out.

It's equivalent to a child who plugs his ears with his fingers and shouts "Nanana, I can't hear you!" when faced with trouble.

How can you ensure that you don't reach that point, especially in sensitive, difficult conversations? You may not be able to, but having the awareness that their impossibility might be accidental or unintentional might take the edge off the tension.

If your difficult conversation partner doesn't seem to want to listen, there are three things that might be at play.

They Might Not Understand

Sometimes, the most obvious explanation is the right one.

If someone is being impossible with you, is it more likely they've decided to completely disregard you as a human being, or that they've misunderstood what you've said?

As Chapter 4 emphasized, it is important to not confuse or combine intent and impact.

They might not be giving you a hard time, they might not have the mental horsepower to understand you or your argument. They just don't have the proper mental resources to process all the facts and issues at play in your negotiation. They're not stonewalling you; you just aren't registering to their sense of logic and they might be too proud to admit it.

When someone can't understand your words, they might reply defensively or make light of your arguments by saying "You're not making any sense," "You're being crazy and stupid," or "You're talking nonsense."

Their statements may be absolutely true to them, but it says more about their inability to understand what's going on and the issues at play instead of any issues with you.

If you find that someone isn't following you and can't understand, stop pushing them to. Just as it doesn't make any sense to try to force somebody who was born blind to see, don't try to force somebody who is too dense.

You must lower your expectations and accommodate them with more time for explanation and examples. You don't want to appear patronizing, but imagine how you might explain a situation in the simplest of terms to a child, step by step, and go from there.

They Don't Want To Understand

The second possibility of someone who appears to be impossible and impenetrable is that they just don't want to understand.

They get what you're saying and can connect the dots logically, but they don't want to arrive at the same conclusion as you. Maybe they're selfish or maybe it doesn't fit their personal agenda. Whatever the case may be, you're feeding them information that they would rather not hear. It's inconvenient, it disappoints them, it deflates their ego, and it definitely irritates them. So they choose to not acknowledge it.

It's easy to spot people like this because they tend to deflect your arguments to a personal issue because they can't deal with it substantively.

Usually, people who don't want to understand will respond with phrases like, "You're getting on my nerves," or "If you keep talking about that you're really going to make me mad."

Don't take this the wrong way. It may seem like they're pointing a finger at you or accusing you, but if you pay attention to what they say, it's about them. They're not saying that you don't make sense. They're just trying to stop your onslaught.

Are there additional reasons they may want to disregard your argument or stance? They are mostly related to being selfish, but here are important aspects: laziness, provocation, cheapness, their own self-esteem, and their belief that they know more than you. Whatever the case may be, these people that simply don't want to understand are a dime a dozen.

These people think that they have everything figured out and if something doesn't fit the narrative, they dismiss it. Again, it's not about you, the sufficiency of your facts, or the strength of your arguments. These people just enjoy a degree of willful denial.

People are often selfish and lazy, so the way you combat someone who doesn't want to understand is to keep pushing them. They're not reacting poorly, they are just avoiding and deflecting. At some point, they will not be able to deflect any longer. There are only so many excuses you can give, and your perspective will win if you keep pushing them.

They Shouldn't Understand

Some people rightfully shouldn't understand what you say to them.

This occurs when you make the mistake of assuming your priorities and views are shared by others.

The person you're trying to reach might understand the point perfectly well, but it's mostly irrelevant and not important to them.

For example, the CEO of a company may try to instill a sense of urgency to the night janitor of the company. The janitor might understand the CEO on a logical level, but it still doesn't matter or register to them because their priorities are so different.

If you're raising a point that really doesn't matter to someone, then the fault is on you. You're trying to push an issue that only affects you, or that you should be dealing with yourself. Just as you are entitled to your own personal priorities, give them enough respect to acknowledge their different priorities. Maybe the issues you're raising simply aren't that important to them.

In this case, others shouldn't understand because you are being petty or irrelevant to their interests.

How do you deal with this type of non-compliance? You let it go. This shouldn't have come up in the first place. You need to focus on what's truly important to you and allow them to do the same. The hard part is recognizing it. Always approach people first by asking yourself, "Why do they care about this?"

Running into the wall of seemingly impossible people is very frustrating.

You have to go back to finding the right battles to fight. In certain areas like business, or anything that can be quantified to hard data and where fairly predictable forecasts can be made, you can win over people that are sitting on the proverbial fence.

However, if you're dealing with soft topics that lean heavily towards biases and opinions like politics, ethics, religion, and philosophy, there is no objective right and you might spend your time merely spinning your wheels.

You need to know when to choose your battles. Sometimes you'll need to battle someone who doesn't want to understand something you find important like your choice of occupation.

In the case of negotiation, it's not worth your time to debate taste and opinion. Time is your most precious asset, so how much of it do you want to spend dealing with impossible people who won't admit you're right even if you've competently debated every step from A to Z?

Chapter 16. Dealing With Counterstrikes

I vividly remember one occasion from an otherwise toasty Christmas of my childhood.

I was with my parents and we had just exited a shopping mall. As you might expect, there was a skinny man dressed as Santa Claus standing near the entrance, ringing his bell for donations.

I told my parents that I wanted to donate, but they told me they didn't have any cash to give Santa. I didn't relent, so my mother ended up digging fifty cents out of her purse and put it into my grubby palm.

I ran over to Santa and put my fifty cents into the bucket he was holding. He looked at me for a second and remarked, "That's the best you can do? Get out of here."

Now, say what you will about the cynicism of Christmas-time charities, but this was a pretty harsh response to a six-year old just meaning to do well. It just goes to show that no matter how well-meaning you are or how solid you think your position is, you will have to deal with counterstrikes.

You'll still have to deal with defensiveness. You'll get people being unreasonable. People will try to pass the blame. You'll wade through passive aggressive behavior. People will lie, threaten, stonewall, cry, be sarcastic, shout, mope, sulk, accuse, or otherwise take offense.

Regardless of how tactful you are and how well you position your argument, you have to be ready for counterattacks.

In order to win and master the art of difficult conversations, you have to deal with counterattacks like professional. Just because you're beyond the combat mentality doesn't mean your counterpart is.

It's very difficult to separate reactive emotion from everything else. Some people simply can't take criticisms well. Others are just truly and profoundly sensitive.

The key to preventing counterstrikes and keeping a difficult conversation civil is to preemptively address feelings of defensiveness before any attacks even begin.

What follows is a five-step process for doing so and making your difficult conversation flow as smoothly as possible.

Step One: Understand

The first step is to understand why people counterstrike. As I mentioned before, people quite frequently come from a place of insecurity and self-preservation.

Being confronted in a difficult conversation puts people into "fight or flight" mode. They aren't often able to run away, so resort to fight mode to protect themselves from danger. There's no physical danger, so what they are most eager to protect is the ego and their sense of pride and self-worth.

You can additionally understand people based on how they counterstrike. It can reveal their specific insecurity that you've unintentionally uncovered. People are usually operating from a stance of fear and prevention.

For example, narcissistic defensive people appear to have an unconscious and extreme fear of being found inferior. Similarly, they particularly hate feeling helpless. This pushes them to take extreme efforts to overcome insecurity. How do they do this? They try to project an air of superiority by insulting and demeaning others. They try to drag you down to their level.

Paranoid defensive people, on the other hand, appear to have an unconscious and extreme fear of being betrayed. It's not that they are actually being betrayed, they just don't want to feel that they're being betrayed or let down. This pushes them to become so insecure that everything seems to be a plot or conspiracy against them. They tend to hold onto unreasonable grudges, and often take the first step in attacking people so they can hurt others before others hurt them.

It's always a good idea to know why people are feeling defensive and why people attack, and trace it back to a base of insecurity. You can't solve a problem if you can't define it. Know where the counterstrikes are coming from.

Step Two: Clarify and Narrow

Now that you understand why people counterstrike and are able to acknowledge that it is not personal to you, the next step is to ease people's insecurities and make them feel safe.

In step two, you are clarifying that you are not a threat to them, and narrowing your issue so that it's not an attack on their whole character. The way they park their car isn't going to escalate to a tirade on how they live their life.

Whatever the case may be, indirectly reference the insecurity to assure them that you are not talking about that, and make your true intentions known.

For example, "No, I know that you're an amazing driver. My parents even told me so! I just want to clarify that I'm only talking about this instance and that you're awesome otherwise."

Spell it out for them that you're not judging their character. You're only talking about a narrow, small issue that is outside of them.

Step Three: Avoid Negativity

The next step is to avoid giving negative feedback.

Any real or imagined slight by a defensive person will easily turn into a counterstrike, or at least playing the victim in an emotional attempt to weaken your position.

Even if someone insults you, you can't drop to their level, because then nothing can be accomplished. As I stated, even if you're not interested in the combat mentality, not everyone will agree with that approach. You should be prepared for it.

When people become negative and counterstrike, it's because they would rather attack you and bide time to figure out whether what you say is true or not – whether their ego can survive intact of not.

Instead, focus on solutions and how you can help this person achieve what they want out of a situation. Look at how they can benefit. Always remember at the back of your head that it's not about them. It's about how they affect other people. If you're able to keep a laser-like focus on this, you will get enough emotional distance so you can successfully avoid giving negative feedback.

Step Four: Time Out

It's important to keep in mind that defensiveness is an emotional reaction that people sometimes cannot help. Their ego and pride get the best of them.

Logic usually prevails in the long run, so the best course of action is to give them time to simmer down. Give them a time out and allow them to snap back to their usual self outside of the fog of emotion.

This way, they can think clearly about the issues you've risen without feeling that they're facing the fire of the moment. The more defensive and egotistical a person is, the more they will need time to cool off to process things.

This approach should carry over in the actual conversation, as well. Allow long silences during your conversation. Allow them to break the silence. Don't interrupt. Be prepared to call another time out if it seems like things are getting too heated, or schedule regular ones.

Step Five: Invoke Empathy

Most normal people are empathetic to a degree in the sense that they don't want to cause harm to others.

Most people are able to step into other people's shoes if you let them know the impact of what they're saying or doing – so that's exactly what you should do.

Let them know that their defensiveness or other tactics like blaming and passive aggression is making you feel like you need to censor yourself. Let them know that their reactions are forcing you to feel like you're walking on eggshells, and this is having an impact on your relationship.

By simply being told how they make you feel, they can take things down a notch. They can conduct themselves in such a way that they minimize the harm that they're causing you.

Most people would be able to relate to this. Most people don't want to be made to feel that they're making someone walk on eggshells. By letting them know this, they can get a clear picture of what's going on. This may have a tremendous impact on their behavior.

You see, people who are used to only blowing up and reacting often get what they want because people simply give up arguing with their emotional reactions. If you're one of the few people that have actually pushed back and spelled out the impact of their behavior on people who are trying to have hard discussions with them, they may realize what's going on change their behavior.

Chapter 17. Becoming Confrontation-Fluent

Becoming fluent in difficult conversations is not only helpful in dealing with argumentative people, it's the key to getting what you want.

No matter how lucky you are in life, there are still difficult conversations you have to endure to get what you want. The most common of these is a conversation with a superior where you ask for a raise or promotion.

Studies have shown that people who simply ask for raises tend to be higher paid throughout their lives.

Taking the chance to talk to your significant other about what bothers you in bed makes you both happier. Studies have shown that conflict resolution is a major factor of successful marriages.

By being mindful of how you deal with people, you increase the likelihood that you can clearly and effectively get the message you're trying to deliver across.

Tip One: Don't Try to Be Right

Whenever you're engaging in a difficult conversation, it's not because you're trying to get them to concede that you're correct. If that's your motivation, you need to re-examine what you're trying to accomplish.

The point of a difficult conversation is not to say that you are right or they are wrong, it's to solve the problem of when you both have been right and wrong.

This is the tone you need to establish early on in the conversation. Leave combat mode for when there are actual conflicts and put on your Sherlock Holmes hat instead.

You must be prepared to not let your ego get in the way. Don't have too big of an ego to avoid helping to solve the situation by admitting that you are wrong. Always be ready to admit your failings.

Tip Two: It *Will* Be Awkward and Uncomfortable

Don't go into a difficult conversation discussion fearing the awkwardness of it.

Oftentimes, that will be the worst consequence, which isn't really that serious.

Assume it will be awkward and uncomfortable. Assume that your palms will be sweaty and your stomach may feel queasy.

The fact is, there isn't a singular phrase that will make those awkward and uncomfortable feelings vanish.

Have the expectation of awkwardness and discomfort and you position yourself to take charge of the situation and roll with the punches.

Compare this with assuming that things will go smoothly. You're essentially setting yourself up for a major disappointment since people don't usually react well when they are told they are wrong, are called out, or feel judged.

The dread you feel at the prospect of a difficult conversation is something you grow used to. Imagine how often a manager at a large company has to let people go or give bad news? Or a doctor, or a surgeon, for that matter?

Things will get better.

Tip Three: Check Your Assumptions

Check yourself to make sure that you're not making assumptions about other people's motives or the other party's intentions. Focus on what they did and the impact of those actions. Leave it at that. Don't try to read in too much into the situation, or speculate on how malicious people are trying to be.

More than we care to admit can be explained away by an unexpected lack of awareness..

When you attribute emotions to people's actions, you become emotionally worked up and create unfair or inaccurate judgments. The more emotionally worked up both of you get, the less likely the conversation will lead to anywhere positive.

Try to divorce emotion from the discussion and focus on objective results instead of reading emotions into what they did or said.

Tip Four: The More You Run, the Bigger Problems Become

If you try to stray away from confrontations or bury your head in the sand, you're only making things more difficult for yourself.

You may have avoided the issue for now, but you can rest assured that when it pops up in the future, it's going to be much harder to resolve. You can only sweep so much matter under the rug.

Deal with problems as they appear.

If you create a pattern of avoiding confrontation, you will be perceived as a doormat and pushover. If you continually fail to draw lines in the sand as to where your boundaries are, you can't blame people for seeing you as a pushover.

Unless you like feeling disrespected regularly, this is not a good option.

Deal with issues head on. Look at confrontations straight in the eye and make sure you have the right skill set to do so.

Tip Five: Confrontation Is Healthy

Aside from the social and psychological benefits of confrontation and difficult conversations, there are physiological bases for them.

For example, studies have shown that anger left unresolved releases cortisol, the stress hormone, in mass amounts, which fatigues your brain and increases retention of fat. Further studies regarding suppressed anger have found that the associated anxiety produces proteins that have the effect of literally shrinking your brain.

If that isn't bad enough, lingering resentments can activate the amygdala, causing us to exist in a kind of permanent fight-or-flight state. You are constantly on edge. You're so stressed out that you're either ready to put up a fight or shrink from the situation. This has the overall effect of eroding your immune system, inflaming your coronary arteries, and triggering a variety of physical problems.

People with high blood pressure, migraines, and frequent headaches can sometimes trace these physical maladies to unresolved personal emotional issues.

You cannot please everybody by simply letting them run over you. That's not going to happen. You have to deal with issues straight on so that you're not bottling up resentment and angst.

According to clinical studies, people who constantly try to please others actually have a higher risk of suffering mental disorders that impact their prefrontal cortex. This can leave them in a stunted state that prevents them from recovering from their emotional and mental trauma.

Don't kick the can down the road. Confront your uncomfortable situations with other people head on. By paying attention to the tips I've outlined, you increase the likelihood that you will end up with a win-win situation or at the very least minimizing otherwise explosive situations.

You don't have to live with unnecessary stress where you end up only punishing yourself. You deserve better.

Chapter 18: Dirty Tactics Defense

It goes without saying that if you've consumed the contents of this book, the arguments you put forth from now on in any difficult conversation are going to be grounded in reality, thought out, and thorough.

Unfortunately, just like with the combat mentality, just because you've decided on a civil method of argumentation doesn't mean the other person has. People can get downright personal and dirty, and the mental gymnastics people sometimes use to justify their statements can be impressive.

Many times, people don't even realize that they are using dirty tactics. In other words, logical fallacies.

A logical fallacy is a pattern of reasoning that sounds logical on the surface, but is actually completely illogical. They are dangerous because they usually have the superficial appearance of reason and logic, and often the people that use them aren't aware that they are using a logical fallacy.

One of the most famous logical fallacies is called the *straw man argument*. A straw man argument is when you rephrase your opponent's argument and then refute it — however, you've purposefully restated their argument incorrectly and falsely.

For example, let's say your opponent states that you advocate no protein and no vegetables, despite the fact that all you said was that you think sugar and fat have their places in a healthy diet. It's an extreme misrepresentation that is logically misleading because that wasn't your argument at all.

I've written extensively on the straw man argument fallacy so I won't repeat it here. Instead, I've described for you four of the most prevalent logical fallacies in difficult conversations, and methods to defend against them.

Sometimes, all it takes is a deeper look into what someone is saying.

Burden of Proof Fallacy

The burden of proof logical fallacy is a misattribution of who needs to prove something in an argument. It assumes that the person who is trying to *disprove* a claim bears the burden of proof, but that is incorrect. The person who first made an assertion is the party who bears the burden of proof.

If we went along with people who use the burden of proof fallacy, the person that spoke first would have the upper hand in any argument because you would need to prove them wrong. Someone could win by silence, which doesn't prove anything, it just means there is a lack of opposition, a forfeit.

To illustrate, let's take the following example. I say that aliens are in fact amongst us hidden as lizards and dolphins. To someone using the burden of proof fallacy, since no one can provide proof that this is 100% not the case, the statement could be considered true and valid. "You can't prove me wrong, so I'm right."

In daily situations, for example, I state that I washed the dishes every day last week. Neither party can prove the validity of this claim, so using the burden of proof fallacy, I would claim victory.

This fallacy relies on peoples' inability to instantly refute any argument.

How do you defeat this fallacy?

Bring up the example that I used just above involving lizards and dolphins. You cannot assume the truth of an argument when proving the truth of the argument.

Start making wild claims about their character, and see how they react when they can't immediately offer proof to the contrary. The best defense against the burden of proof fallacy is to use it against them so they realize what their stance is in actuality.

Middle Ground Fallacy

The middle ground fallacy is when someone characterizes the middle point between two perspectives as the truth in the matter.

This is sometimes true, and the third story often seeks to find it. But the middle ground fallacy takes it a step too far by assuming that the midpoint of any two arguments is the truth.

For example, I might say that wearing green causes people to think far more clearly. My friend disagrees and states that she has read a study where the color of your clothing does not affect mental faculties. Someone using the middle ground fallacy would say that wearing green only moderately improves focus, as opposed to a lot or zero.

As you can see, the middle ground fallacy invents an argument from nothing. It appears to be logical because it takes both stances into consideration, but it generates what is equivalent to gibberish in the scope of the arguments. The midpoint usually has no relation to arguments unless it's an argument about the temperature of the bath water.

How do you defend against the middle ground fallacy?

Ask what the relevance of the midpoint is to the arguments. Highlight the fact that the midpoint only exists as a point of reference, and doesn't have any substantive value. It is only conceptually a compromise, not the literal interpretation.

Beg the Question Fallacy

The beg the question fallacy is where someone makes an assertion because they believe the conclusion to be true. It is circular reasoning, and is like a power cord plugging into itself. There is no basis for the conclusion.

Let's say I claim that a certain singer is the most popular person in the world because everyone knows their name.

It's a statement that almost makes sense because it is consistent, but really means nothing since the conclusion is given in the assumption. People use the beg the question fallacy in the hopes of validating an assumption they believe in strongly but has no logical foundation. This fallacy is used by those who likely feel cornered and can't think of anything else to say.

How do you defend against the beg the question fallacy?

By asking question after question about their statement.

So why is the singer popular? Why does everyone know them? I thought it was because they were popular? But isn't that because everyone knows them?

Dig a deep hole for them and see how they try to get out of it. Make it clear that they are repeating themselves as opposed to presenting evidence.

Slippery Slope Fallacy

The slippery slope fallacy is probably one you have used before. I know I have

The slippery slope fallacy is when someone assumes a long sequence of events will be inevitable by allowing a particular situation to unfold. It's used frequently in politics to try to increase the impact of how people vote on certain issues. They operate on the fear of far-off consequences.

For example, take this common political talking point: if you take away our guns, we will become a weak nation and other countries will invade us within the next two years.

The slippery slope fallacy is based on a series of assumptions that probably aren't true, and are typically sensationalized. Where is the logical connection between taking away guns and becoming a weak nation? Subsequently, what is the logical connection between becoming a weak nation and other countries invading us?

It's quite a stretch to believe that something akin to an invasion will transpire from relinquishing citizens' firearms. And yet, that's what users of the slippery slope would have you believe. It's a fear-based response.

How do you defend against the slippery slope fallacy?

By doing what I just did: attempt to draw the logical connections first from A to B, then B to C, and so on. Slippery slopes often take you from A to Z, glossing over the steps involved in between. Call them out on what would actually need to happen, and if the end result is motivated by fear or logic.

Conclusion

I've come a long way since encountering that janitor who kept parking in my assigned parking space. Thank goodness.

How would I have handled that situation differently? Well, there are over 20 changes from this book I could have made to my behavior to save myself a serious case of stress and rage.

I believe the parking spot situation perfectly illustrates why difficult conversation skills will elevate you above others. These are situations that occur nearly every day of our lives. Most people don't understand the correct response to them, and thus are held back, bit by bit, every single day.

It's tough allowing avoidance and passive aggressiveness to dictate your life. It's time to seize control back and get what you want from the people in your life!

Sincerely,

Patrick King
Social Interaction Specialist
www.PatrickKingConsulting.com

P.S. If you've enjoyed this book, please don't be shy. Drop me a line, leave a review, or both! I love reading feedback, and reviews are the lifeblood of Kindle books, so they are always welcome and greatly appreciated.

Other books by Patrick King include:

CHATTER: Small Talk, Charisma, and How to Talk to Anyone

Speaking and Coaching

Imagine going far beyond the contents of this book and dramatically improving the way you interact with the world and the relationships you'll build.

Are you interested in contacting Patrick for:

- A social skills workshop for your workplace
- Speaking engagements on the power of conversation and charisma
- Personalized social skills and conversation coaching

Patrick speaks around the world to help people improve their lives as a result of the power of building relationships with improved social skills. He is a recognized industry expert, bestselling author, and speaker.

To invite Patrick to speak at your next event or to inquire about coaching, get in touch directly through his website's contact form at http://www.PatrickKingConsulting.com/contact

Cheat Sheet

Chapter 1. The Why of Difficult Conversations

Learning to deal with difficult conversations in tactful ways means that you can move your life forward without running away from situations that are tense and awkward.

Chapter 2. Grant Emotional and Logical Validation

One of the first steps of a difficult conversation is to grant the other person emotional and logical validation. Let them know that you can walk in their shoes and that they have valid points.

Chapter 3. Find the Third Story

Your story is only your interpretation, and the other person has their version entirely. But the truth is in between as the third story. Seek this out and you will find where the miscommunications lay.

Chapter 4. Separate Impact from Intent

The impact of someone's actions should not be interpreted as an intent to cause that impact. Oftentimes, they are not even remotely related. Assume, at worst, neutral intentions and your interpretation of the events will be much softer.

Chapter 5. Address Causation

Instead of addressing the main pain of the moment, dig deeper to address the causation and underlying flaws so the situation you have found yourself in never surfaces again.

Chapter 6. Tact(ics): Speak So People Will Listen

There are no perfect lines for you to use in a difficult conversation, but there are certain ways to speak so people will listen. Tact, refraining from using "you" statements, and listening over speaking are just some of those ways.

Chapter 7. Tact(ics): Speak To Create A Dialogue

The purpose of a difficult conversation is to create a dialogue to solve a problem, not point fingers. Using a criticism sandwich and using only the bare minimum of negativity that you need to make your point are some of the ways to do this.

Chapter 8. Choose Your Battles

You can't complain about every negative situation you find yourself in, or else you will be the boy who cried wolf. Think to yourself: is this a situation that has repercussions, will repeat itself, or crosses your boundaries?

Chapter 9. Create Safety

You can't expect people to open up to you emotionally if they don't feel safe to be vulnerable, so you have to create that space for them. Emphasize non-judgment and be the first to be vulnerable.

Chapter 10: Be Solution-Oriented

For maximum productivity, establish a framework to find a solution to the problem instead of focusing on the problem. Work to move forward and know the kinds of solutions that you want.

Chapter 11. The Five Phases To Difficult Conversations

There are five phases to any difficult conversation that should be followed. Breaking the ice, your story, their story, the third story, and finding a mutually beneficial solution.

Chapter 12. Feedback With Grace

There is an optimal way to give and receive feedback, and it involves using the Losada ratio of positivity and negativity and knowing the overall purpose of feedback, which is to improve and enrich and never to insult or indulge.

Chapter 13. Know BATNA And WATNA

The BATNA and WATNA are negotiation terms. What do you expect the best result to be in your life if you avoid a difficult conversation, and what do you expect the worst result to be? Can you live with the best result from avoidance, and are you prepared for the worst result from avoidance?

Chapter 14. Negotiation Tactics

A negotiation and a difficult conversation have the same goals, essentially. The most effective ways of getting what you want, perhaps at the expense of the other party, Is to focus on their secondary wants and pressures. Sometimes the best way is through the side door.

Chapter 15. Dealing With Impossible People

There are three types of impossible people: those who can't understand you, those who don't want to understand you, and those who shouldn't understand you. There are certain tactics to push past each type of person to make them understand.

Chapter 16. Dealing With Counterstrikes

Understand what drives people counterstriking. It's almost always related to ego and pride, and the perceived threat to the ego and pride.

Chapter 17. Becoming Confrontation-Fluent

Being comfortable and accepting confrontation as a part of your life will lead to greater happiness, health, and better relationships.

Chapter 18: Dirty Tactics Defense

People may not realize the errors in their logical arguments, so it's up to you to catch them and point them out. The logical fallacies I cover (and detail how to defeat) are the burden of proof fallacy, beg the question fallacy, middle ground fallacy, and slippery slope fallacy.

Made in the USA
Middletown, DE
15 March 2017